*Newcomers* SERIES

# Immigrate to Canada
# A Practical Guide

**Nick Noorani**
Best-selling author "Arrival Survival Canada"
**and Catherine A. Sas, QC**

**Self-Counsel Press**
*(a division of)*
International Self-Counsel Press Ltd.
USA    Canada

Self-Counsel Press acknowledges the financial support of the Government of Canada through the Canada Book Fund for our publishing activities.

Printed in Canada.

First edition: 2014

**Library and Archives Canada Cataloguing in Publication**

Noorani, Naeem, 1957-, author
    Immigrate to Canada : a practical guide / Naeem "Nick" Noorani and Catherine A. Sas.

(Self-Counsel newcomers series)
Issued in print and electronic formats.
ISBN 978-1-77040-209-6 (pbk.).—ISBN 978-1-77040-958-3 (epub).—ISBN 978-1-77040-959-0 (kindle)

    1. Emigration and immigration law—Canada--Popular works. 2. Canada—Emigration and immigration—Handbooks, manuals, etc. I. Sas, Catherine A., author  II. Title.  III. Series: Self-Counsel newcomers series

| KE4454.N66 2014 | 342.7108'2 | C2014-905603-6 |
| | | C2014-905604-4 |

**Self-Counsel Press**
*(a division of)*
International Self-Counsel Press Ltd.

| Bellingham, WA | North Vancouver, BC |
| USA | Canada |

# Contents

## 16  Your First Steps in Canada

## 17  Cost of Living in Canada

# Notice to Readers

Laws are constantly changing. Every effort is made to keep this publication as current as possible. However, the author, the publisher, and the vendor of this book make no representations or warranties regarding the outcome or the use to which the information in this book is put and are not assuming any liability for any claims, losses, or damages arising out of the use of this book. The reader should not rely on the author or the publisher of this book for any professional advice. Please be sure that you have the most recent edition.

**Note:** The fees quoted in this book are correct at the date of publication. However, fees are subject to change without notice. For current fees, please check with the court registry or appropriate government office nearest you.

Prices, commissions, fees, and other costs mentioned in the text or shown in samples in this book probably do not reflect real costs where you live. Inflation and other factors, including geography, can cause the costs you might encounter to be much higher or even much lower than those we show. The dollar amounts shown are simply intended as representative examples.

Website links often expire or web pages move, at the time of this book's publication the links were current.

# Dedication

Writing a book like this cannot happen without many people. We would like to acknowledge the tremendous support of our families and teams for their enthusiasm, patience, encouragement, resilience, and, most of all, ceaseless assistance in completing this book.

Special thanks to my wife, Sabrina, for helping edit, format and reformat, and then once again reformatting the book!

To my friends: Margaret Jetelina, Alla Gordeeva, Debbie Catherwood, and Ana-Maria Gheorghiu.

To Pacifico Restaurant for being a welcome haven providing us both with nourishment and Wi-Fi!

To my granddaughter, Laila — the first Noorani born in Canada! The first generation plants the trees for the second generation to enjoy the shade.

— Naeem "Nick" Noorani

To my Great Grandparents and Grandfather Paul who immigrated to Canada from Russia and Poland to give all of my family a better life.

To my husband, Paul, who immigrated to Canada to be with me.

To my sons, Louis and William, who remind me every day of the significance of assisting people through the Canadian immigrant journey.

A big thanks to the Miller Thomson Vancouver immigration team for their editing assistance — Victor Ing, Puneet Mann, Judy Solinap, Fred Li, and Tanya Wilson.

— Catherine Sas

# Foreword:
# A Message from Senator Yonah Martin

Nick Noorani is an award-winning Canadian immigrant, who, by his example, demonstrates the best of Canada and the opportunities that Canada affords to each immigrant.

Thank you, Nick, for writing this book to share the wealth of your immigrant experiences with others preparing to experience Canada themselves.

May all who read this book be blessed with greater insight and knowledge for a successful immigrant life in Canada.

At your service,

The Honourable Yonah Martin
Deputy Leader of the Government in the Senate
yonahmartin.sencanada.ca

# A Word from the Authors

It has been 16 years since I first landed in Canada, and it has been a journey of tremendous challenges and wonderful discoveries. Born in Mumbai, India, I had a terrific career in advertising and marketing, working with some great companies and people. Like most parents, my wife, Sabrina, and I wanted to give our children the best in the world. With my family in tow, I moved to the Middle East (Muscat, Abu Dhabi, and then Dubai) to seek my fortune.

A few years later, it was Sabrina who suggested that we move to Canada. With my brother already here, we knew a little bit about the country, or at least we thought we did. We felt it was the right place for us to build a new life, not only for ourselves, but for our children and our future grandchildren. We no longer wanted to be just "visitors"; we wanted to settle in a place we could call home. We weren't alone in this sentiment; most newcomers to Canada come with similar dreams and hopes for their future as "Canadians."

We applied for immigration under the Federal Skilled Worker category and received our letter of acceptance a few months later. Back then, it was easier to get into Canada, even though the wait time was still lengthy. Since coming to Canada, I have been working with immigrants helping them find their success. The first step was a book my wife and I coauthored called *Arrival Survival Canada*, which is now in its third edition published by Oxford University Press; it's a Canadian bestseller (http://arrivalsurvival.com/).

You could consider *Immigrate to Canada* as a prequel to *Arrival Survival Canada*. While that book goes into everything you need to know in your first year after arriving in Canada, this book concentrates on how to get here, and some of the initial steps you need to take before and after you arrive.

Over the years, I have met thousands of immigrants face to face through my "7 Success Secrets for Canadian Immigrants" seminar and on the streets of Canada. In 2012, I did ten seminars in five cities in India speaking to hundreds of brilliant professionals who wanted to come to Canada but didn't know where to start!

Skilled workers who want to migrate to Canada often fall victim to fraudulent immigration consultants, paying huge fees with no results. Even legitimate immigration lawyers and consultants will cost you a lot of money with no guarantee of getting you approved to come to Canada.

I wanted to create a level playing field for prospective immigrants. I wanted to write a book that would be a quick and simple read for immigrants who could use the information to apply themselves, and learn pertinent information on Canada at the same time.

Several reports have shown that immigrants who do not do their research prior to arriving have a harder time settling here!

My "Know Before you Go!" program and "Prepare for Canada" (http://www.prepareforcanada.com/) website provide a wealth of information to prospective immigrants. Please do use it!

Catherine Sas is a well-known Canadian immigration lawyer and a friend of mine, so when I asked her about contributing to this book, she responded enthusiastically.

Immigration policies change all the time and it's important to keep on top of new policies and rules, so Catherine and I have included web links for the programs so if there are any changes, you always have the latest information!

Immigrating to Canada means so many things to so many people. All immigrants, be they skilled immigrants, students, or temporary workers have one thing in common — dreams of a better tomorrow for themselves and their families. Welcome to the beginning of your Canadian dream! I hope this book helps you on your journey to Canada.

— Naeem "Nick" Noorani
www.nicknoorani.com

As an immigration lawyer, I have been assisting immigrants and their families to settle in Canada for more than 20 years. The immigrant journey is far more than coming to a new country. It is a complicated application process that may take many years; it is the leaving of familiar territory to a strange new one; and it is an emotional journey of resettling and adapting to a new homeland.

While Canada is a welcoming country, the immigration experience can still be a challenge. This book is meant to demystify that ever-changing process by explaining the various avenues for immigration as well as important tips for arriving and settling in Canada.

Naeem "Nick" Noorani has experienced firsthand becoming a Canadian. These pages offer considerable insight to the immigrant experience. The immigrant's story is Canada's story: Its past, its present, and its future, and it will be Canada's future for many years to come. May this book smooth the process of immigration for you. Nick and I will also keep you informed with regular updates and new editions found at www.canadacountdown.ca.

— Catherine Sas, QC

## What This Book Will Do For You

With so many different programs, finding the correct category to apply is critical to getting your visa approved! This book will help you with the following:

1. Provide you with the detailed information you need to know to determine if you are eligible and how to successfully apply.

2. Cut through government jargon so Canada's immigration process is easier to understand.

3. Provide an overview of what immigrating to Canada will actually be like — challenges and all!

4. Save you money by helping you apply and arrive!

5. Help you choose which immigration category to apply to your situation.

# Abbreviations

**ADR:**     Alternative Dispute Resolution

**CBSA:**    Canada Border Services Agency

**CELPIP:**  Canadian English Language Proficiency Index Program

**CIC:**     Citizenship and Immigration Canada

**CLB:**     Canadian Language Benchmarks

**COPR:**    Confirmation of Permanent Residence

**CPC:**     Case Processing Centre

**CRA:**     Canada Revenue Agency

**DMP:**     Designated Medical Practitioner

**EI:**      Employment Insurance

**ELT:**     Enhanced Language Training

**ESL:**     English as a Second Language

**FCRO:**    Foreign Credential Referral Office

| | |
|---|---|
| **FLE:** | Français Langue Étrangère |
| **GST:** | Goods and Services Tax |
| HST: | Harmonized Sales Tax |
| **IELTS:** | International English Language Testing System for English |
| **IAD:** | Immigration Appeal Division |
| **ID:** | Immigration Division |
| **IELTS:** | International English Language Testing System |
| **IRB:** | Immigration Refugee Board |
| **ICCRC:** | Immigration Consultants of Canada Regulatory Council |
| **LINC:** | Language Instruction for Newcomers to Canada |
| **LMIA:** | Labour Market Impact Assessment |
| **NOC:** | National Occupation Classification |
| **PNP:** | Provincial Nominee Program |
| **PR:** | Permanent Resident |
| **PST:** | Provincial Sales Tax |
| **RPD:** | Refugee Protection Division |
| **RPO:** | Refugee Protection Officer |
| **ROPR:** | Right of Permanent Residence Fee |
| **SIN:** | Social Insurance Number |
| **TEF:** | Test d'Évaluation française |

# 1

# The Basics of Coming to Canada

*" ... what keeps the earth turning are the thousands*
*of immigrants walking to new destinations every day,*
*pushing the planet around and around with their*
*millions of footsteps."*

— ANONYMOUS

I still remember my first day in Canada like it was yesterday. It was a chilly day in April of 1998. My family and I were moving from Dubai so we didn't have warm jackets, but my brother who had migrated two years earlier had the car heater on so we didn't feel cold. My first view of the North Vancouver mountains made me fall in love with the place I was to live.

It took a lot of research and planning before I finally settled. In this book I want to share the basics of what I learned with you.

For starters, the organization handling all the applications and issues regarding immigration and citizenship is called Citizenship and Immigration Canada (CIC). This federal department determines immigration policy in Canada, works to ensure all applicants (i.e., temporary workers, international students, and permanent residents) get competent and fair decisions, and also strives to make immigrants first steps toward integration easier. It also offers assistance and protection to refugees and other persons in need.

On the CIC website you can download all the application forms you need to apply for coming either temporarily or permanently to Canada as well as information on how to complete and submit them and payment of the applicable fees.

You can also contact the closest visa office to your city for information on applying for immigration. Visa officers work in Canadian embassies, high commissions, and consulates around the world to process applications for immigration, refugee resettlement, temporary resident visas, study, and temporary work permits. See the CIC website for visa office locations (www.cic.gc.ca/).

---

**Tip:** Be sure that you follow the specific instructions for the visa office serving your country.

---

Completing an application form is one thing; getting it approved is entirely different. The number of applicants far exceeds the number of people approved for immigration. Applying to immigrate can be riddled with an endless stream of complicated forms and confusing requirements. Together with Vancouver, British Columbia-based immigration lawyer Catherine Sas, QC, we have streamlined all the information on the immigration process to Canada.

Note that immigration policies are always changing! It's important to keep on top of new policies and rules, so Catherine and I will keep you informed with regular updates and new editions to this book found at www.canadacountdown.ca.

When you arrive, I'll keep guiding your journey with my best-selling guide to your first year in Canada, *Arrival Survival Canada* (www.arrivalsurvival.com). You may also want to read *365 Tips for Newcomers: Your First Year in Canada*, published by Self-Counsel Press.

## 1. The Changing Canadian Immigration Environment

For someone who immigrated five years ago, Canada's immigration landscape has been completely transformed. Catherine has people coming into her office and asking to do things which no longer exist and fighting with her about why they can't be done the way they want! Our readers need to be prepared for changes to the system.

Here are some of the changes:

- Citizenship and Immigration Canada (CIC) wants to make assessing applications fast and transparent so it is requiring objective third-party services to evaluate language skills and educational qualifications. Applicants will need to have the results of these evaluations before submitting an application. This will enable applicants to see whether they qualify from the outset of the process.

- CIC is going electronic. More and more applications are being made online. This trend will continue but it may have potential challenges. You have to be sure you understand the entire online application process. Make sure that you have a complete copy of your application and supporting documents before you submit them. Once you hit "send" your application is gone to CIC cyberspace.

- CIC wants to be able to process applications quickly and manage its workload, which could mean the end of wait-lists. Expect to see annual caps on the number of applicants eligible in all program categories.

The Minister has also introduced two new immigration programs and announced a third:

- **The Federal Skilled Trades Program:** In order to address Canada's shortage of tradespeople, this new program allows certain skilled tradespeople to come to Canada under their own unique program

- **The Start-up Visa Program:** This new business program is the first of its kind "in the world," as described on the CIC website, by granting immediate permanent residence to promising entrepreneurs who are selected by and matched with approved industry partners.

- **Express Entry Program:** This program will commence in early 2015. Express Entry will transform Canada's immigration program from a passive/responsive system, to a new active recruitment model that will prioritize processing for people with the skills to succeed in Canada.

On May 1, 2014, federal Minister of Citizenship and Immigration, Chris Alexander, introduced the latest changes to the Federal Skilled Worker category. The Minister increased the total number of applications in this category to 25,000 through to April 30, 2015, in 50 different occupational categories with a 1,000 sub-cap for each occupation.

You should also be aware of the following changes:

- Language proficiency is now the single most important factor to qualify under the skilled worker category. A principal applicant can earn up to 24 points for his or her first official language and a further four points for his or her second language for a total of 28 points out of a required 67. Points are now allocated for a spouse's language proficiency rather than education. The message is clear; Canada needs immigrants who can communicate effectively in one of the two official languages — English or French. This overall emphasis on language proficiency can also be seen in the Canadian Experience Class (CEC), Live-in Caregiver, Skilled Trades, and Citizenship programs. Expect this to continue.

- There is a new focus on younger immigrants. The old system gave ten points to anyone between 21 to 49 years of age and continued awarding points until age 53! The revised selection grid will favour younger immigrants by awarding a maximum of 12 points for applicants aged between 18 to 35; one point will be deducted per year after age 35.

- The number of points allocated for past (foreign) work experience will be reduced to 15 from 21. The rationale for this change is that research reveals an ongoing difficulty in transferring work experience from different countries. Concurrent with a reduction of points for foreign work experience is an increase of ten points in the adaptability category for one year of Canadian work experience.

- To achieve speedier processing objective-testing services will be required for both language proficiency as well as educational credential evaluations. Applicants will need to include a language test as well as an education credential evaluation at the time the application is submitted.

- Permanent Labour Market Opinions (LMO) are now called Permanent Labour Market Impact Assessments (LMIAs).

## 2. How Immigrants Can Succeed in Canada

I'm often asked by immigrants, social workers, government officials, and members of corporations how immigrants can succeed in Canada. Every year, approximately 250,000 immigrants come to Canada with dreams of a better life. Most of them have educational qualifications exceeding the Canadian populace but are unable to get employment commensurate with their education and work experience. Some arrive here, but they have to start from the bottom, get retrained, and suffer in "survival" jobs at first.

Corporate Canada, with a few notable exceptions, has not been successful at integrating immigrant talent into its workforce. Part of the challenge has been a shift since the 1990s from European-based immigration to an Asian- and South Asian-dominated immigrant base, which has resulted in companies struggling to understand new immigrants' cultural nuances. With the risk-averse nature of Canadian employers, it's easy to see why professional immigrants are often on the outside looking in. However, some immigrants do make it. So what is the difference between those who do and those who don't?

Having worked with immigrants for the past 15 years, I have observed huge differences between immigrants who succeed and those who fail. While I often talk about success secrets for immigrants, I want to look at this question from the flip side: Why do immigrants fail?

Here are a few pointers that I hope will prompt a better understanding of what can actually help create positive outcomes for immigrants:

- **Know before you go!** I have met immigrants who say, "I am deciding between living in Toronto or Ontario." Toronto is a city in the province of Ontario! This statement demonstrates a clear lack of understanding about the country this immigrant wants to call home! I find it hard to accept that a professional immigrant lands here without having done adequate research not only about the cities, but the professional barriers he or she will face. This is precisely the reason we decided that if you are thinking of moving to Canada, you should have information on your new country (see Chapter 15).

- **Have realistic expectations.** Most immigrants I have met expect to land a job immediately in a company at the same level as their home country. I tell them to be realistic and to think about how long it took them in their home country to get the position they had.

- **Understand your strengths and weaknesses.** I'm talking about language proficiency, soft skills, and corporate etiquette. Note that many immigrants come to Canada with a 90:10 ratio of technical skills to soft skills (see section **2.1** for more information about soft skills). Canadian employers want 40 percent technical skills and 60 percent soft skills but many newcomers can't seem to accept this reality.

- **Embrace change.** I have met hundreds, even thousands of immigrants, and what amazes me is their reluctance to use their geographic change to create other changes. What worked "back home" will probably not work here. A study conducted in 2013 at York's School of Human Resource Management found that immigrants who embraced change were more likely to succeed.

- **Do not become a victim!** The honeymoon period for immigrants lasts a few weeks, which are typically spent sending résumé after résumé in response to job postings. Immigrants go to a settlement centre and learn about Canadian résumé writing and networking. While they are going through this, the immigrants look at their shrinking bank balances and the fear sets in. That fear leads to anger and, in a short period of time, immigrants get into a "victim" mentality, full of anger for a system that doesn't recognize immigrant qualifications.

- **Avoid rearview mirror driving.** The next stage is when an immigrant takes a job not commensurate with his or her qualifications. The immigrant now gets frustrated with his or her lot in life and in order to redeem some of his or her waning self-esteem, he or she spends time talking to everyone about what his or her life was like back home. Often this leads to the person packing his or her bags and leaving Canada.

- **Move out of ethnic silos.** Unable to deal with the newness of interacting with Canadians, many immigrants gravitate toward their own communities where they feel more secure in their language and culture. These ethnic silos hold immigrants back, preventing successful integration with the larger populace. More importantly, it disallows immigrants the ability to work in a multicultural environment.

- **Create new networks.** When immigrants migrate, their networks in their new country are primarily either relatives or friends they know from back home. Most immigrants tend to be unfamiliar with the concept of networking, but without it, they are missing out on key information and potential opportunities.

- **Canada is different.** Canada is not the United States of America. It is also very different from your home country. You must understand that what worked in your home country will not work in Canada.

There is good news! The labour shortage propelled by an aging population and a declining birthrate was put on hold for a while because of the economic downturn between 2008 and 2010. The shortage hasn't gone away, however, and corporations and businesses across Canada, especially in the natural resources category, are facing a huge demand for skilled labour. Immigrants will continue to be the leading source of labour for Canada in the coming years.

## 2.1 Language barriers and soft skills

When I immigrated to Canada, I had a distinct advantage as English was my first language. I went to a good private school so my basic grounding in grammar and writing skills stood me in good stead. However, I spoke a different dialect of English when I arrived in Canada. I now speak Canadian English. There are several words we pronounce differently in India because of the obvious British influence.

From the time I started on this roller coaster journey working with immigrants 15 years ago, I saw that language (or lack thereof) was the single largest barrier for immigrants. I met with engineers, accountants, human resources specialists, among others. Yes, they "spoke" English, but not at the level that their professions needed. When an employer had to choose between a native

English or French speaker and someone who obviously struggled with the language, no prizes for guessing who won!

However, it wasn't just about the language skills. It expanded to soft skills. Research showed that Canadian employers wanted more soft skills than technical skills as the latter people always picked up on the job. A research study conducted some years ago between immigrants and Canadian employers showed a marked disconnect in how employers view immigrants and vice versa. While an overwhelming majority of employers found language skills and soft skills were a barrier for immigrants in the workplace, immigrants did not see this as a problem!

"Soft skills" is a term you will hear quite often in Canada. What does it mean? To help define it, let's first look at the term with the opposite meaning, "hard skills." Hard skills are all the technical know-how, credentials, and experience you have in your field of expertise. For example, if you're a chef, your hard skills are cooking, know-how with kitchen equipment, and so on. An employer looking for an experienced chef will want to know the candidate's abilities in the kitchen, where he or she studied and trained, and any other important credentials.

What would the chef's soft skills be? They are all the intangible qualities that aren't as quantifiable. For example, how does the chef work in a team? Does he or she have good leadership skills? Is he or she organized, dependable, punctual, and friendly? When we are talking about immigrant soft skills, perhaps the most important question is: Can he or she communicate well in English? Unfortunately, many immigrants don't fully understand or want to accept the importance of soft skills in getting ahead in Canada.

My suggestion is to read about developing soft skills or download it for free on the Prepare for Canada website (http://www.prepareforcanada.com/working/nine-soft-skills/nine-soft-skills-no-immigrant-should-be-without/). Note that you will need to sign up as a member to get this and more valuable information.

## 3. Immigration Categories

If you know for certain that you want to call Canada home, you will be faced with the challenging and often confusing task of applying for permanent immigration. There is not just "one" way of coming to Canada permanently.

Note that Canada's immigration program has gone through tremendous changes in the past several years. If you have friends or relatives who have immigrated to Canada in the past five years or longer, it is almost certain that the process has changed since then. Be sure to become familiar with the current immigration process.

There are several classes of immigration under which you can apply. It is important to choose your category wisely, as there are many intricate rules and regulations for eligibility. If you apply under a class for which you are ineligible, you will find it difficult if not impossible to switch categories midstream, which will delay the process and you will incur additional expenses. You need to ensure that you meet the eligibility criteria so that you are certain you qualify for that category of immigration. The following are the leading immigration categories:

- Federal Skilled Worker Class

- Business Immigration Program

- Provincial Nominee Programs

- Family Class

- Canadian Experience Class

- Federal Skilled Trades Class

Each category has its own set of procedures and criteria that we will explain in the following chapters. However, what is common for all types of applicants (together with their dependants) is that they must undergo a medical exam and a criminal record check (see Chapter 3).

While you are able to apply for immigration on your own, if immigrating to Canada is really important to you, it's wise to seek help from a qualified immigration lawyer or consultant to help you navigate the application process (see Chapter 4).

# 2

# Coming to Canada Temporarily: Workers, Live-in Caregivers, and International Students

If you only want to come to Canada temporarily as a worker, caregiver, or student, the process can be much faster than applying for permanent immigration. Many people choose to first come to Canada with temporary status, before deciding on immigrating permanently. If you're not totally sure about moving permanently, starting off with a temporary visa could be the right choice for you.

The Canadian government has found that people who come to work in Canada prior to immigrating tend to integrate better into the community, as they already have stable employment and have had an opportunity to become familiar with the Canadian way of life. As a result, there are now special categories of immigration for those who have been here temporarily such as the Canadian Experience Class (CEC) and Provincial Nominee Program (PNP).

> **Caution:** If you come to Canada with a visitor visa, you cannot change your status to student or worker from within Canada. You need to apply for a visa as a worker or student *before* you come to Canada.

# 1. Working Temporarily in Canada

Canadian employers often seek temporary workers to fill labour shortages or to bring in international expertise. While many of these jobs would be considered low-skilled work, in areas such as agriculture, manufacturing, and hospitality, these are not the only opportunities available. In fact, many temporary workers come to work within skilled and professional industries.

In most cases, you will need a job offer from a Canadian employer before applying for your work permit. Some Canadian employers recruit overseas, but you can also approach Canadian employers through your own research. In some instances, Canadian immigration regulations allow for open work permits, which are not specific to an employer. The most notable of these programs is the International Experience Class (IEC), which allows young people to come to Canada to both travel and work. See Citizenship and Immigration Canada's (CIC's) website for more information on all types of work permits.

## 1.1 Applying for your temporary visa

In order to work in Canada temporarily, it is necessary to obtain a work permit. When applying for a work permit, you will have to show you qualify to work in Canada via one of the following:

- Have a Labour Market Impact Assessment (LMIA) from Employment and Social Development Canada (ESDC) showing that your employer can hire a foreign worker.

- You fall under a bilateral trade agreement such as the North American Free Trade Agreement (NAFTA); Canada has such agreements with Chile, Peru, and Colombia which allow for the exchange of workers and is currently negotiating with other countries.

- Inter-company transferees. For example, if you work for an international company, you can transfer to the Canadian company.

- Provincial Nominee Program (PNP) nomination certificate.

- You are part of a youth-exchange program such as the International Experience Canada (IEC) class, also referred to as the Working Holiday Visa, Young Professional, and International Co-op Programs.

In all of the cases listed here (except for the IEC), you will need an employer prior to applying for a work permit (www.cic.gc.ca/english/work/apply-how.asp). To see if you need a Labour Market Impact Assessment (LMIA), go to CIC's website (www.cic.gc.ca/english/work/apply-who-permit.asp).

## 1.2  Securing a position with a Canadian employer

It can be quite difficult to get a job in Canada while you are in your home country. Given Canada's booming oil and gas exploration industry, there has been some overseas recruitment for technical professions. As Canada's labour requirements grow, employers are scouting international job boards.

In the future, Citizenship and Immigration Canada (CIC) wants to allow employers to search a government database of résumés in a proposed program called Express Entry (EE). This system will be in operation in early 2015. (See Chapter 12 for more information.)

The EE program (www.cic.gc.ca/english/immigrate/express/express-entry.asp) shows promise for job seekers worldwide. In principal, you will register your résumés on a Government of Canada authorized website and employers can interview suitable candidates with a job offer. Prospective immigrants will complete an online form indicating their "interest" in coming to Canada as permanent residents. The form may include information that relates to language proficiency, work experience, and assessed education credentials.

---

**Caution:** Beware of consultancy companies promising jobs along with visas. Many of them are immigration consultants who are not permitted by the Canadian authorities to do recruiting. While there are some reputed firms who are conducting interviews online and hosting job fairs in various countries, they are not permitted by Canadian law to charge you a fee for this.

---

In addition, you must also do the following before being granted a temporary worker's visa:

- Satisfy a visa officer that you will leave Canada at the end of your work permit.

- Show that you have enough money to support yourself and your family while you are in Canada.

- Respect the law and have no criminal record.

- Show that you are not a risk to the security of Canada.

- Be in good health (you may have to have a medical examination).

---

**Note:** If you or a family member has a criminal record, you may not be eligible for either a temporary visa or permanent residence or you may have to apply for Criminal Rehabilitation.

---

Generally, temporary work permits are issued for a period of one to three years. During that time, many temporary workers decide that they want to live in Canada permanently. Some may apply for permanent residence independently through the skilled worker category as long as they satisfy the current criteria. Alternatively, others who have worked in Canada may pursue permanent residence through the Canadian Experience Class (CEC).

Furthermore, some employers will find that the workers they have brought into Canada are of such value to their companies that they will choose to nominate them through a Provincial Nominee Program (PNP). Each of these processes for permanent residence will be described more fully in the subsequent chapters.

Find out more about working in Canada temporarily on CIC's website (www.cic.gc.ca/english/work/apply-who.asp).

## 2. Caregiver Program

There is a special temporary worker program called the Caregiver Program. Caregivers provide care for children, elderly persons or persons with disabilities in private homes. (Formerly called the Live-in Caregiver program, it was recently changed as of Nov. 30, 2014.)

To work as a caregiver in Canada, you must make an application to the visa office for a work permit (www.cic.gc.ca/english/work/caregiver/index.asp). If your application is successful, you will receive a work permit. To be eligible, you must have the following:

- A positive Labour Market Impact Assessment (LMIA) from an employer in Canada.

- A written contract with your future employer, signed by you and your employer.

- Successful completion of the equivalent of at least one year of Canadian post-secondary school education.

- At least six months approved training or one year of full-time paid work experience as a caregiver or in a related field or occupation (including six months with one employer) in the past three years.

- Knowledge of English or French at the "initial intermediate" level at Canadian Language Benchmark (CLB) 5 as confirmed by a designated third party language test. (See Chapter 5, section **1.1**).

- A work permit before you enter Canada.

Applicants in this category are usually interviewed by Citizenship and Immigration Canada (CIC). It is important that you prepare thoroughly and know as much as possible about your future employment in Canada. Even though you most likely have never been to Canada, you will be asked questions about your employer, your family, your job duties, and where you will live. Be prepared!

After you have completed 3,900 hours of authorized full-time employment under this program within four years of your arrival, you can apply for permanent resident status. There are, however, certain requirements and restrictions in calculating these hours and becoming eligible for permanent residence, including a medical check. Fortunately the program has been improving in recent years including the elimination of the live-in requirement as well as the introduction of an open work permit that allows caregivers to find other employment so they can have more than one job or employer.

---

**Note:** On October 31, 2014 the Minister of Immigration Chris Alexander announced changes to this program including the elimination of the live-in requirement along with speedier processing times for permanent residence applications. For more about the changes to the Caregiver Program see: http://news. gc.ca/web/article-en.do?nid=898719.

---

## 3. The International Experience Canada (IEC) Program

The International Experience Canada (IEC) program is the new name for familiar programs known as the International Youth Program and International Exchange Program. Both of these programs allowed for the exchange of young people to come and visit

Canada and work to support themselves while they visited and became familiar with the country. The Canadian government approved the creation of an international travel and exchange program in 1967 to allow for the exchange of young people between partner nations to enhance relationship building between those countries. The IEC program is more commonly known as the Working Holiday or Young Professional Work Permit program.

The IEC program is a two-step process: The first stage is the IEC assessment to see whether you meet the eligibility criteria (this is an online process). If you meet the criteria, you will be issued an IEC conditional acceptance letter. Stage two is to apply for a work permit with the conditional acceptance letter.

Canada has agreements with 32 different countries to permit young people to apply for work permits under the IEC. Every agreement is different with respect to the type of agreement and the category of eligibility such as the Working Holiday, Young Professional, or International Co-op program and each has different eligibility requirements such as age limits, duration of the permit, or whether or not it can be renewed. In addition to the country specific agreements, there are also some organizational arrangements that are recognized under the IEC that are able to provide work permits for youth such as the Student Work Abroad Program (SWAP). Check the Canada Immigration website to find out all the categories that are available under the IEC program.

To submit an IEC application, there are two steps. First, you need to meet the program requirements for the IEC as set out on CIC's website. Second, you need to meet CIC's requirements to apply for a work permit (www.international.gc.ca/experience/intro_incoming-intro_entrant.aspx?lang=eng&view=d).

In order to be eligible to apply, you must be a citizen of one of the countries with which Canada has a bilateral agreement. Some of these agreements require that the people be living in their country of citizenship at the time they make their application; whereas others allow applicants to submit their application to the Canadian visa office responsible for the country in which they are residing.

Check whether there is a program for your country and follow the specific instructions to apply for an IEC work permit on the regional visa website for the geographic region for which you are a national or in which you reside. Most visa offices only accept applications for a limited time each year. The timing and process for submitting applications under the IEC is different for each country. It is important to check the visa office website for your country regularly and follow the guidelines set out on the website for your particular visa office.

For many young people, the IEC category is a good way to pursue permanent residence in Canada. Most IEC programs provide for work permits that are for 12 months or more, which means you can obtain the one year of work experience required to apply for permanent residence under the Canadian Experience Class (CEC). For those agreements that only allow for a work permit of less than 12 months, it still provides you with a wonderful opportunity to connect with a Canadian employer who may be willing to offer you further employment in the future, ultimately leading to permanent residence.

While a work permit under the IEC may permit you to lawfully work in Canada, possession of the work permit alone will not make you eligible to apply for permanent residence in Canada. If permanent residence is your ultimate goal, you will need to gain full-time work experience in Canada for a minimum of 12 months to be eligible to satisfy the CEC criteria. You must also obtain work experience in an occupation as described in the National Occupational Classification (NOC) at NOC levels O, A, or B. Semiskilled or low-skilled work experience at NOC level C or D will not qualify for permanent residence under the CEC. See the Employment and Social Development Canada (ESDC) website for information about the National Occupational Classifications. (www.esdc.gc.ca/eng/jobs/lmi/noc//index.shtml).

Furthermore, you need to ensure that your work experience is in an occupation that will qualify for permanent residence under the CEC class. Recent changes to the program have deemed certain occupations ineligible to apply (see Chapter 10 for more information).

In December 2012, CIC introduced the bridging work permit to allow applicants for permanent residence in certain classes to be eligible for a bridging work permit. This is good news for IEC workers who have applied for permanent residence status, been found eligible to make that application, but are reaching the expiration date of their IEC work permit. This new bridging work permit will allow you to obtain a further work permit to remain in Canada while your permanent residence application is finalized. In order to qualify for a bridging work permit, you must meet the following criteria:

- Be in Canada.

- Have a valid work permit due to expire within four months from the time of application.

- Have received a positive eligibility decision on your permanent residence application.

- Make an application for an open work permit — submit form IMM 5710: Application to Change Conditions, Extend My Stay or Remain in Canada as a Worker (http://www.cic. gc.ca/english/information/applications/extend-worker.asp).

# 4. Studying in Canada

Canada is a very popular destination for international students who want to obtain a North American education. Canadian colleges and universities are very welcoming of foreign students as they enrich the campus experience for Canadian students.

Once your decision to come is made, the next steps may not be as simple. There are many issues to consider, starting in your country of origin before you leave, considerations in Canada after you arrive, and the application process itself.

## 4.1 How to get your study permit

Before applying to a college or university, students should first take a language test such as the International English Language Testing System for English (IELTS) or Test d'évaluation de français (TEF) for French, in order to determine if you have sufficient English or French proficiency to meet the school's requirements. These test results may be useful later on in applying for permanent residence status. It is important to check with the school to see what type of language test it requires. Language test requirements may vary for study purposes and immigration purposes. Make sure you take the test necessary to obtain a letter of acceptance from the school. Most universities and colleges have an international studies department that can provide all the information you will need to be accepted at the school.

After the language test, the next step is to obtain a study permit. In order to do that, you must first apply to a Canadian school, generally a college (Colleges and Institutes Canada: www.accc.ca) or university (Association of Universities and Colleges of Canada: www.aucc.ca), and obtain a letter of acceptance.

Once you are issued a letter of acceptance from the school, it is necessary for you to make an application to a visa post abroad for a study permit and further demonstrate that you or your family have sufficient funds to cover the cost of the tuition as well as living expenses for the duration of your studies in Canada.

In addition, it is advisable to include a study plan, which is an explanation of the reason you want to obtain an education in Canada and what your long-term objectives are in obtaining this education. The study permit application process can often take several months so it is advisable that you complete the application at least four or five months before your courses are due to commence.

## 4.2 Choosing a postsecondary school

Canada's schools are as diverse as its population, from internationally recognized universities such as the University of Toronto, University of British Columbia, and McGill University, to medium-sized colleges and universities as well as private technical and language institutes, including English as a Second Language (ESL) schools.

Universities focus on the development of critical thinking and research skills as students work toward a bachelor's (undergraduate) degree, a Master's (graduate) degree, or a PhD (doctorate) degree. Class sizes tend to be large, with some lecture halls counting hundreds of students although attending smaller tutorials or labs may also be part of the class requirement. Many universities also offer student housing, and lots of extracurricular and sport activities. Tuition costs are highest at universities.

Colleges and technical institutes offer a range of applied programs that are typically focused on preparing you for a career. At one of these types of schools, you will probably be working toward a diploma, a certificate, an applied degree, or transfer credits toward a university program. Some colleges also offer apprenticeship training for the trades (e.g., carpentry, electrical). The hybrid "university college" may also offer undergraduate degrees. Classes range in size, but are typically smaller than in universities. Tuition rates are also less expensive than universities.

Private career colleges are private businesses that could be either for-profit or nonprofit. They do not receive government funding like publicly funded colleges and universities, so fees may be quite high. They offer certificate and diploma programs in many fields such as business, electronics, and health services, with flexible learning schedules, enrolment at many different times during the year, and compressed programs that deliver training over a short time. Some private institutions, including some English language schools, are not regulated by the government so be sure to do plenty of research before you pay. You want to ensure that the school you are attending is recognized by CIC so that you can obtain valuable work experience both while you are attending classes as well as after graduation.

Canada Immigration has recently introduced a list of designated learning institutions. In order to be able to study in Canada, you must have a letter of acceptance from the designated learning institution. A list of these designated learning institutions at the postsecondary level is available on CIC's website (www.cic.gc.ca/english/study/study-institutions-list.asp).

## 4.3 When and how to apply

Each educational institution has its own deadlines and rules for admission. Some schools run on a three-semester basis, and accept students at the beginning of each semester, while others run on a yearly schedule, with application deadlines in early spring. Note there is also generally a non-refundable admissions fee you must pay when submitting your application.

Contact the admissions department at your school of interest for more information. You can also obtain more information about what programs the school offers and requirements for admission in its calendar or on its website. Generally, there is a minimum level of language proficiency in order to be accepted.

Each school will have its own criteria for recognizing international academic qualifications. It may have certain requirements for the translation and authentication of your academic credentials. You may be required to have your academic credentials assessed through one of the following credential evaluation services:

- Ontario: World Education Services (www.wes.org/ca)

- Alberta: International Qualifications Assessment Service (http://work.alberta.ca/immigration/international-qualifications-assessment-service.html)

- British Columbia: International Credential Evaluation Service (www.bcit.ca/ices/)

- Canadian Information Centre for International Credentials (www.cicic.ca)
- Alliance of Credential Evaluation Services of Canada (www. ca nalliance.org/brochure.en.stm)

Such agencies charge a fee so make sure the school will accept an assessment done by one of these independent agencies. As of May 4, 2013, all skilled worker applicants for permanent residence will have to have their education credentials assessed by an independent education credential evaluation service. New evaluation centers have been designated by the federal government and can be found on the Government of Canada's website (www.cic.gc.ca/english/immigrate/skilled/assessment.asp). This may also affect the credentials evaluation process for postsecondary educational facilities.

## 4.4 Taking ESL courses while attending other programs

If you came to study at a university or college, English as a second language (ESL) classes may be something you want to consider as well. Even though you're busy attending classes in your field of study, if your English (or French) isn't good enough to easily understand the professors or to write clear essays and assignments, your education in Canada could suffer.

Learning the language is one of the most important strategies for success in a new country. Even if you plan on staying in Canada for only short-time studies before returning to your homeland, it is a smart idea to brush up on your language skills.

Check with your university's continuing education department to see if it offers ESL for adults. If not, check with smaller, public and private colleges. Generally, the free ESL classes available at immigrant settlement agencies are reserved for permanent residents.

## 4.5 Cost of tuition

Tuition fees vary from school to school, and even program to program. Tuition for universities will be higher than colleges, just as tuition for graduate studies will be higher than for undergraduate.

Tuition fees will be the bulk of your academic expenses, but not your only costs. Count on paying for various administrative and student fees as well as books for each course. If you need housing, it will be another large expense to add to your costs.

Make sure you have enough money for all your basic needs or requirements. As mentioned earlier, there are some limitations on working in Canada as an international student. Also note that international students are not typically allowed student or bank loans in Canada.

## 4.6 Arranging housing

The ideal situation would be to have prearranged student housing on campus before you arrive in Canada. It's convenient and adds to that "university experience," but it can fill up fast and comes with certain restrictions. Costs vary depending on the institution, as do types of housing — from shared rooms to independent studios to family units. Note that not all postsecondary institutions have campus housing; generally, only the larger universities do. Check with your school to find out more information about student housing.

If you had no luck in securing on-campus student housing, your next option is an off-campus rental. Depending on how much you have to spend on rent, you can look for the following:

- A room to rent in a house (with shared bathroom and kitchen) is around $400 or more per month.

- A separate suite in a home (often a basement suite) is around $600 or more per month.

- A bachelor or one-bedroom apartment in an apartment building is around $600 or more per month.

Many students also look for a roommate to share accommodation. In some cases, two or three roommates together could even afford to rent a small house with three bedrooms, which would cost upward of $1,000 per month. Of course, rental costs vary widely across the country and between cities, so these prices are general estimates. Some rentals include the cost of electricity, heat, and water, and sometimes even have cable included. Finding furnished accommodation is also possible. Also note that some landlords will require you to sign a lease and pay a damage deposit or first and last month's rent.

To find available rentals, look in the newspaper classifieds, on bulletin boards at your school, and on the Internet. Some campuses have webpages dedicated to helping students find off-campus housing such as the University of Ottawa (http://www.residence. uottawa.ca/en/och/).

## 4.7 Off-campus and postgraduate work permits

The Canadian government has recognized that when students have obtained education in Canada they integrate very well into the Canadian workforce and can provide valuable skills to the Canadian labour market as well as make ideal permanent residents. Accordingly, there are several ways for students to gain work experience, both while studying in Canada and after graduation.

Students are able to work part time while they are pursuing their studies. Previously, this was through the Off-Campus Work Permit Program. This program required that students attend their program of study at a designated college or university on a full-time basis for at least six months and that following this initial six-month period they were able to work 20 hours per week during school and full time during school breaks until the completion of their studies. However, this has changed and for the better!

As of June 1, 2014, it is easier for international students to gain work experience in Canada. Students attending a designated learning institution on a full-time basis are able to work up to 20 hours per week while attending classes. Currently your study permit entitles you to work on a part-time basis while studying full time. You are also permitted to work full time during class breaks such as the summer and holidays. This gives international students an opportunity to get valuable Canadian work experience while completing their studies.

Students in Canada attending designated learning institutions are now able to work without a work permit and start immediately. Once students have a study permit, they may work up to 20 hours a week and only for the duration of their educational program. During school breaks and summer or winter holidays, students are eligible to work on a full-time basis. Students must be in full-time attendance at a designated learning institution (see the list of eligible schools: www.cic.gc.ca/english/study/institutions/participants.asp).

Following graduation, students are then eligible to apply for a Post-Graduation Work Permit of up to three years duration, depending on the length of their course of studies. The course of studies must be full time and at least eight months long in order for students to qualify. This is an open work permit, and students can work in any field either full time or part time. Part-time work may affect your ability to apply for permanent residence; for example, the Canadian Experience Class (CEC) requires students to have one year of full-time work experience which is defined as being a minimum of 30 hours per week. If you are working part time, you will need to have two or more part-time jobs that provide you with at least 30 hours or more of work per week. Students who apply for the postgraduate work permit must do so within 90 days from receiving written confirmation from their school that they have completed their studies and are eligible to receive a degree or certificate. Also, your study permit must be still valid.

## 4.8 Moving toward permanent residence

It is good to remember that work experience after graduation may lead to permanent residence status. Students who have studied in Canada and then worked in Canada on a full time basis for one year are eligible to apply for permanent residence through the Canadian Experience Class (CEC). Furthermore, students who are working on Post-Graduation Work Permits often develop relationships with their employers and have an opportunity to prove themselves, and many employers choose to nominate them for permanent residence status through the Provincial Nominee Program (PNP).

International graduate students who have obtained their PhD degree in Canada are eligible to apply for permanent residence status through both the Federal Skilled Worker Program as well as through many Provincial Nominee Programs (PNP). Most PNP graduate student programs accept Master's students. In many cases, postgraduate students will not require an employer or work experience and are able to apply for permanent residence merely on the strength of their graduate education. Find out more about studying in Canada on CIC's website (www.cic.gc.ca/english/study/index.asp).

> **Note:** The permanent resident program for CEC, PNP, Federal Skilled Workers, and Federal Skilled Trades are all designated to become a part of Canada's new Express Entry program starting in early 2015. Stay tuned for these new changes and how they may affect international students seeking to become Permanent Residents. (See Chapter 12 for more information about Express Entry.)

# 3
# Mandatory Requirements, Fees, and the General Process

There are several different immigration categories, which will be discussed in the following chapters. What's important to understand in this chapter is that every category has its own set of procedures and criteria; however, what is common to all types of applicants (together with their dependants) is that they must undergo a medical exam and a criminal record check.

## 1. Medical Exam

The purpose of the medical exam is to protect the public health of Canadians and to avoid putting too big a strain on the health-care system. You can find the list of the authorized medical practitioners (also known as "panel physicians") for each country and territory on the Citizenship and Immigration Canada (CIC) website (http://www.cic.gc.ca/pp-md/pp-list.aspx).

It is important to note that the results of a medical exam are only eligible for one year, so if your visa isn't issued within this time period, you will have to take another medical exam. You must arrive in Canada while your medical exam is still valid.

You do not take the medical exam prior to the application process. Once CIC has assessed your application for eligibility requirements, you will be sent medical examination forms for you and your family. You must go to a designated medical practitioner (DMP) to take the exam and the doctor will forward the results to CIC. A DMP is a doctor who has been designated and trained by CIC to complete its medical examinations.

# 2. Criminal Check

The criminal check (also known as a "police certificate") ensures that an applicant does not have a criminal record and is not likely to pose a threat to Canadians.

You will need a criminal check document from each country or territory where you have lived for a period of six months or longer since the age of 18. Those who have worked or studied outside of their home country for longer periods of time, or those who are currently living away from their home country for whatever reason, must take special notice of this. If you cannot obtain a police certificate, you must provide a written explanation to Citizenship and Immigration Canada (CIC). As in the case of medical exams, criminal clearances are only valid for one year.

Police certificates that are not in English or French must be submitted together with a translation of the original certificate (not a photocopy) made by an accredited translator.

It is up to you to make all the necessary arrangements to obtain your police certificates and send them to CIC. It will also do a security check on your behalf directly with the countries you have lived in, but you will not have to do anything for this.

For US applicants, you will need to provide a Federal Bureau of Investigation (FBI) check as well as a state police clearance for each state that you have lived in for more than six months since you were 18 years of age.

> **Note:** If you have, or a family member has, a criminal record, you may not be eligible for permanent residence or you may have to apply for Criminal Rehabilitation.

# 3. Application Fees

All immigration applications require payments of proscribed fees to accompany the applications on submission. Be sure to follow the payment instructions for the type of application that you are making as set out in the Citizenship and Immigration Canada's (CIC) website. It does not accept personal cheques and, in many cases, does not yet accept credit card payments. Make sure you include the correct fees for you and your dependants with your application.

> **Note:** If you fail to include the correct fee payment, your application will be considered incomplete and returned to you.

The immigration process has many expenses, some that are expected such as application and processing fees, while others are optional or unanticipated, such as hiring a representative or being required to attend an interview. The reality is that immigrating to Canada is expensive. There are considerable expenses that you need to be prepared for in the process of preparing your application. Here are some of the expenses:

- **CIC application fees:** These are the application-processing fees that the CIC charges for your application for permanent residence (or visitor, or student, or work permit). It is very important that you include the correct application fees when you submit your application. If you fail to include the appropriate fees with your application, it will be considered incomplete and returned to you. Under some classes of applications, fees can be paid online; in others they must be mailed with your application. Look for the addition of online filing options in the future.

- **Right of Permanent Resident fee:** CIC charges a fee for the permanent resident visa for you and your dependants. Generally, CIC asks for the fee payment at the end of the process when it is ready to issue your visas. However, it can be paid at any stage of the application process — at the time of submission or anytime thereafter. Paying the Right of Permanent Resident Fee at the outset of your application can save a few weeks or months of processing time. In the event that your application is refused, the fee is refunded to you.

- **Hiring an immigration lawyer, consultant, or paralegal:** You may wish to have a professional assist you with your application. This can cost several thousands of dollars. Many representatives charge flat-rate fees and others charge by the hour. Be sure that you have a clear idea of what this will cost and that it is set out in writing. (See Chapter 4.)

- **Supporting documentation:** The cost of obtaining the supporting documents to your application can be expensive as well. You will need to include a wide variety of supporting documents including transcripts, educational certificates or records, bank or financial documents, tax returns and financial statements, phone records, and photographs. There may be a cost to obtain this material in addition to the cost of photocopying.

- **Medical examinations:** You and your family members will need to undergo a medical exam by a designated medical practitioner (DMP). It costs a few hundred dollars. If your application takes several years to process, you may be required to undergo and pay for a second set of medical examinations.

- **Criminal record checks:** Every person included in your application that is 18 years of age or older will need to include a criminal record check or police clearance for each country that they have lived in for more than six months since they were 18 years of age. You may have to provide updated clearances if your case takes longer than a year to process.

- **Interview costs:** In some instances, CIC will want to interview you or your family members. You may be required to travel to the visa office responsible for your geographic region. This may require significant transportation costs as well as hotel expenses. You will also need to obtain a qualified independent interpreter if you are not able to communicate effectively in English or French.

- **Moving expenses:** Understandably the cost of moving to Canada is significant. You not only need to arrange for travel to Canada for yourself and your accompanying family members, but also for the transportation of your personal belongings and household effects. Be prepared for this significant expense!

> **Caution:** Keep in mind that permanent resident visas cannot be extended. If you fail to enter Canada before the visa expires, you will have to begin again with the whole application process and pay the fees again! If you don't have enough time to settle all your affairs in your country of origin before the expiration of your visa, you can always come to Canada and become a permanent resident and then go back to your country of origin to settle everything and then return to Canada later.

## 4. General Information about the Application Process

The application process may differ slightly between each category, so more information on how to apply will be included in the subsequent chapters. However, there are some commonalities in the process for all potential immigrants: download the forms, complete them, pay the fees, and mail the application.

### 4.1 Downloading and completing the forms

The forms for all classes can be downloaded from Citizenship and Immigration Canada's (CIC) website (www.cic.gc.ca). Do not panic if you made any mistakes when filling in your information because you can download the forms as many times as you wish, for no charge.

There is a validation process for many types of applications. It is important to ensure that all the information is correct before validating and printing a copy of your application for your records and before you submit it electronically. Be sure to print a copy of your application before you hit the send button as you will be unable to get a copy of it once it is submitted.

If the application is incomplete, unsigned, illegible, or does not meet the criteria, it will be returned to you. Many people opt to get help from immigration lawyers or consultants in completing their application forms to ensure no errors are made (see Chapter 4).

If you're completing your application forms online, take note of a new addition to CIC's application procedure — the introduction of barcode-generating application forms. This means that after completing the application form, you will have to press the "validate" button on the form and print a page with barcodes on it. The validate button will capture electronically all the information you have typed onto the form and submit it to CIC. Should you need to change any information in the form, you would need to validate the form again to ensure that the accurate information is submitted. You will need to have the latest version of Adobe Reader installed on your computer and your JavaScript settings turned on.

## 4.2 Review your application before sending

Be sure that all the information in your application is true and correct. If you provide inaccurate information in the application, you may be found to have committed misrepresentation and your application will not only be refused, but you will be unable to submit any kind of application to Citizenship and Immigration Canada (CIC) for a period of two years. (**Note:** New legislation will increase this to five years.)

People often make the mistake of deleting or not including information that they think is not relevant to the type of application they are making. This can be found to be misrepresentation. It is better to disclose all the circumstances you may be concerned about and let the officer determine the significance of the information. Examples of such irrelevant information may relate to driving infractions (potential criminality), incomplete education, and non-marital relationships.

Failing to disclose the existence of family members can be even more serious and may result in a permanent prohibition in being able to bring your family members to Canada. Be sure to disclose all family members, spouses, and children — including those born out of wedlock or persons that you have lived with outside of marriage — as they will be considered to be your relatives under Canada's Immigration laws.

If you are using the services of an immigration lawyer or consultant, be sure to disclose everything to your representative so that he or she can advise you on how to present any difficult information. Always tell the whole truth. If your representative advises you to conceal information or provide false information, you should stop working with that person immediately. It is an offence for lawyers or consultants to counsel or advise people to put false information in their immigration applications. However, CIC will hold you accountable for the information provided in your application. It is not an acceptable explanation to say that you relied on a paid representative. You are responsible for the information contained in your application so make sure it is accurate. Insist that you see a final draft of your application prior to it being submitted. Your lawyer or consultant should also give you a complete copy of your application for your records.

The following are some quick reminders about the application process:

- Sign and date your application. Unsigned applications will be returned. Ensure you have read it first. Never sign any documents that you haven't read.

- Validate your forms. Save and print a copy of all the forms. If you make any changes you will need to re-validate the forms.

- Make sure that all the documentation and information requested are provided with your application and are clear and legible.

- Notify the visa office handling your application of any changes in your information (e.g., address, telephone number, marital status) and birth of any children. If your marital status changes, or you welcome another child after receiving your visas, you must advise CIC *before* coming to Canada. Bringing a family member to Canada who has not been included in your application may result in a loss of your permanent resident visa.

- Do not make any unnecessary inquiries to the visa office. The progress of your application can be checked online on CIC's website once you receive your file number. Go to the "Check My Application Status" webpage (www.cic.gc.ca/english/my_application/status.asp).

- Have your documents translated into English or French by a certified translator.

- Keep a copy of all forms and documents submitted with your application.

## 4.3 What happens when the application is approved?

If the application is approved, you will be asked to send your passport to the Canadian visa office where you applied, in order to receive the permanent resident visa. You will also get a Confirmation of Permanent Residence (COPR) document that you must have with you when you enter Canada, along with a valid passport.

When you arrive at the point of entry to Canada, you will have to present your COPR document and visa to a Canada Border Services Agency (CBSA) officer. Make sure to pack your documents in your hand luggage and have them easily accessible.

If you are bringing more than $10,000 with you in whatever form, you must disclose this to the officer. Failure to disclose your funds may result in a fine, confiscation of the funds, or even imprisonment.

If the CBSA officer decides that all your papers are in order, he or she will authorize you to enter Canada as a permanent resident. You will also receive a useful guide with important information for newcomers. Your Permanent Resident Card will be mailed to you (usually after four to six weeks) at the Canadian address written on the COPR, so make sure that the address is correct. You will be given a copy of your COPR document. Make sure you keep your COPR in a safe place as you will require this to renew your permanent residence status and/or apply for citizenship.

# 4
# Legal Representation

Immigrating is such a big step, and with such high stakes, it is no wonder the market is full of consultants and companies that promise to help you in establishing your new life in Canada.

As an immigration applicant, you can apply on your own, hire an immigration lawyer, or use the services of an authorized immigration consultant or paralegal (paralegals are only authorized in Ontario). In Quebec, you can also hire notaries who are members of the Chambre des notaires du Québec.

Applying on your own is the least expensive way. You can download all the necessary forms and instructions from the Citizenship and Immigration Canada (CIC) website at absolutely no cost. If you are confident in your ability to understand the instructions and you are certain that you meet all of the necessary criteria for the type of application you are submitting, then there should be no problem to apply by yourself. You can also seek help from friends and family, as long as they do not charge you a fee.

However, making any mistakes or omissions on your application can cause your application to be denied, which makes it that much harder to re-apply. It's critical that your application is completed accurately and according to CIC's requirements the first time around.

# 1. Hiring Representation

When you choose a paid immigration representative you have to be very careful. Unfortunately, there are many scammers who take advantage of potential immigrants. Most of these scams are online, but you can also find them in newspaper ads, flyers, and sometimes even in offices that have a respectable appearance.

Since these unscrupulous individuals make very tempting promises, you should be aware of the following tell-tale signs of an immigration fraudster or scammer:

- **Guarantee the acceptance of your application:** No one can give you that guarantee. Only Canadian government officials in embassies, high commissions, and consulates have the power to accept or reject your application, and even they cannot guarantee anything before processing your file.

- **Promise a certain time frame:** "Live and work in Canada by July!" Beware of any such claims. A consultant or representative has absolutely no influence on how fast your application will be processed. The Citizenship and Immigration Canada (CIC) website has posted some general time frames that you can expect, but even these are not definite.

- **Promise that you will not need certain documents:** "No criminal checks or medical exams required!" There is no such thing. All applicants older than the age of 18 have to provide a criminal check or police certificate and undergo a medical exam.

- **Give the illusion they have special "connections" at embassies and consulates:** No one has special access, and such a promise is 100 percent false.

The easiest way to find out if an immigration representative is authorized is to check if he or she is a member in good standing of one of the following organizations:

- A provincial or territorial law society for immigration lawyers or paralegals (paralegals are recognized to provide immigration services only in Ontario so far).

- The Chambre des notaires du Québec for Quebec notaries.

- The Immigration Consultants of Canada Regulatory Council (ICCRC) for consultants.

> **Note:** See the Resources at the end of this book for the contact information of these organizations.

The Canadian government does not accept representations from paid representatives who are not authorized, and will return your application if this is the case. It is an offence for anyone other than an authorized representative to provide immigration advice for a fee. The government has enacted legislation regarding who is authorized to give immigration advice in order to protect the public (see "IP 9 — Use of Representatives" at www.cic.gc.ca/english/resources/manuals/ip/ip09-eng.pdf).

Applicants must declare if they have used the services of an authorized representative to obtain immigration advice or assistance in preparing an immigration application. It is the obligation of the applicant to ensure that the representative is authorized. That means that you are responsible to determine that any representative that you hire to assist you is lawfully authorized to do so.

Since representation services are usually costly, it is best to double check and find out more about the reputation of a representative. You can contact the Better Business Bureau (www.bbb.org) to see if there are any complaints made against the person as well as the Law Society, the Chambre des notaires du Québec, and ICCRC. Also, ask your representative to provide references and to share more about his or her training and experience.

## 1.1 Should you choose a consultant or lawyer?

What is the difference between a lawyer and consultant? Both an immigration lawyer and immigration consultant can assist you with your application, but only the lawyer can appeal a case in Federal Court if your application is rejected.

When starting off with either type of authorized representative, you should have a written contract that clearly stipulates the services offered and the fees. Also, you should get a signed receipt anytime you make a payment toward the fee.

Be careful about leaving any original documents with the representative. Citizenship and Immigration Canada (CIC) does not generally ask for original documents, except for the criminal check or language test results (and their translations). In most cases notarized copies of original documents will be satisfactory.

Do not sign any blank forms or documents that you do not understand because you are legally responsible for anything that carries your signature. Remember to fill in the name and contact information of your representative on your application form because there is no other way for CIC to see that you actually authorized this person to represent you.

An honest representative should do the following:

- Show transparency and not hesitate to answer all of your questions.

- Keep you updated with the progress of your application.

- Send you copies of any documents and the complete application that he or she prepares for you.

- Never ask you to complete or sign false forms containing misleading information.

You are entitled to change your representative, or simply cancel his or her services, as long as you notify CIC in writing about it.

## 1.2 Unpaid representatives

You can be represented by a family member, friend, or member of a non-governmental organization or religious organization, as long as there are no fees exchanged. In order for an unpaid representative to be recognized by Citizenship and Immigration Canada (CIC), you need to provide written consent by filling in form IMM 5476 — Use of a Representative (http://www.cic.gc.ca/english/information/applications/representative.asp).

# 2. Filing a Complaint against Your Representative

If, for some reason, you are displeased with the services of your authorized representative, there are several ways to get help. Citizenship and Immigration Canada (CIC) does not assist you in disputes with your representative unless the latter has broken an immigration-related law (e.g., if the representative submitted fraudulent documents in your name). If this is the case, you must immediately notify the CIC office that is dealing with your application or the Canada Border Services Agency (CBSA) (www.cbsa-asfc.gc.ca).

If the reason for your dissatisfaction is not of an immigration-related nature (e.g., if the representative did not provide all the services for which you paid), you can file a complaint with the regulatory body to which the representative belongs (see a list of contacts in the Resources section at the end of the book).

If your complaint is about an employee of an authorized representative, discuss the situation with his or her employer first. If no satisfactory measures are taken to address the situation, you can file a complaint at the representative's regulatory body.

In case you hired and paid a non-authorized representative (in other words, if you fell into the trap of a scammer), notify the law enforcement agency where the representative lives. Non-authorized persons can advise you about your application process, but cannot represent you or charge you a fee.

## 3. You Are Responsible for Your Information

Remember that even if you use the services of an authorized representative, you are ultimately responsible for all of the information in your application, and ensuring it is accurate. Even if you have a representative, it is your responsibility to review the application and know its contents.

This can't be stressed enough: It is against the law to give false or misleading information to Citizenship and Immigration Canada (CIC). If the information on your application is false or misleading, you may be refused entry to Canada or be deported from Canada. Immigration representatives who tell you to provide false or misleading information are also breaking the law.

# 5
# Federal Skilled Worker Class

Coming to Canada as a federal skilled worker has traditionally been the most popular route of entry to the country. What most applicants don't realize is that the application process is increasingly restrictive. Someone who was eligible ten years ago may not make the cut today. That's because too many of the skilled workers who came here for better lives were sorely disappointed. They did not find the opportunities and success they had anticipated in their field of expertise.

While most recent immigrants have educational qualifications exceeding the Canadian populace, many are still unable to get employment commensurate with their education and work experience. Some of the reasons immigrants fail include the following:

- They are not properly prepared prior to arriving.

- Their language skills are inadequate.

- They don't have the proper soft skills (e.g., communication, interpersonal, presentation skills) that Canadian employers expect.

- They have unrealistic expectations.

- They have a victim mentality.

- They are resistant to change and they don't accept they must adapt to the way things are done here.

In recent years, Citizenship and Immigration Canada (CIC) has modified, and will continue to modify, the requirements of the Federal Skilled Worker Class of immigration to improve immigrants' chances for success in Canada. The newest version of Canada's Federal Skilled Workers' (FSW) program was introduced in May 2013 revamping the criteria for selection under this category. The most recent changes to the program came into force on May 1, 2014. The focus of ongoing changes to the FSW program is to enhance a new immigrant's chances of integrating into the Canadian workplace as quickly as possible by placing greater emphasis on age and language ability of both the principal applicant and his or her spouse. The Minister of Immigration posts changes regularly. Be sure to regularly check the FSW program criteria to see if you are eligible to apply.

In recent years, CIC only considered applications from skilled professionals and tradespeople who had experience in a certain list of proscribed occupations and who could prove that they could adapt economically in Canada (http://www.gazette.gc.ca/rp-pr/p1/2014/2014-04-26/html/notice-avis-eng.php). The FSW remains restricted to specific occupational categories.

This immigration class does not handle cases of professionals who wish to immigrate to Quebec, as Quebec has its own skilled workers' program.

> **Note:** As of January 1, 2015, the FSW program will become a part of the new Express Entry program (see Chapter 12).

# 1. Eligibility and the Point System

In order to be eligible to apply as a skilled worker, you must meet the following requirements:

- Have adequate work experience in one of the listed eligible occupations.

- Meet a points' score of 67/100.

- Provide the results of an official language proficiency test.

- Provide an evaluation of your educational certificates.

For further details about approved language-testing services or educational-verification services please see the Government of Canada's webpage "Have Your Education Assessed — Federal Skilled Workers" (www.cic.gc.ca/english/immigrate/skilled/assessment.asp).

If you do not meet the eligibility criteria, do not submit an application as a federal skilled worker; instead, check to see if you satisfy criteria in the other classes.

If you meet the requirements, your application will then be assessed on a points' system, in which you earn points based on the following six selection factors:

- Language ability.

- Age.

- Education.

- Work experience.

- Adaptability.

- Arranged employment in Canada.

If you have a score lower than 67, it is not recommended that you start the application process as your application will likely be denied. It is better to work on certain aspects (e.g., studies, work experience, and language) so you can achieve a better score in the future.

You can estimate your potential score based on the points system information in the following sections. If you plan to immigrate with your spouse or common-law partner, you should both calculate your scores, and choose the one with the highest score to be the principal applicant.

## 1.1 Language

Language is now the most important factor under the skilled worker criteria. Language proficiency is crucial because it can bring you a maximum of 28 points. Unlike the other selection factors, this is one that you can improve in a relatively short time in order to increase your score. If you speak both English and French, you must choose one as your first official language, preferably the one you know best. Your proficiency will be assessed based on your ability to speak, read, write, and listen.

Citizenship and Immigration Canada (CIC) assesses proficiency in accordance with the Canadian Language Benchmarks (CLB) standards. Note that the CLB is not a test, it is a language-proficiency descriptor that visa officers use based on the evidence you provide (e.g., points scored on language tests).

Applicants can score language points based on the following criteria:

- **CLB/NCLC 9 (Fluent):** Participates in business meetings and debates. Understands a broad range of general and abstract topics. Writes formal and informal notes and summary documents.

- **CLB/NCLC 8 (High):** Understands technical conversations and reading material in their line of work. Asks questions, and analyzes and compares information in order to make decisions.

- **CLB/NCLC 7 (Moderate):** Understands the main points and important details of a conversation and can write routine business correspondence. Able to participate in small group discussions and express opinions and reservations about a topic.

In order to determine whether your score meets CLB standard for fluent, high, or moderate proficiency, you can check CIC's website (www.cic.gc.ca/english/immigrate/skilled/language-testing. asp). Table 1 shows CIC's points system for language proficiency.

You will be awarded four points for your second official language if you meet a moderate proficiency level (CLB 5) in each of the four language skill areas.

In order to prove your language proficiency, you must take a language test. In English there are two approved tests:

- The International English Language Testing System (IELTS) (http://www.ielts.org/test_takers_information.aspx).

- The Canadian English Language Proficiency Index Program (CELPIP), which is available only in Canada (www.celpiptest. ca).

## Table 1
## FEDERAL SKILLED WORKER POINTS SYSTEM FOR LANGUAGE PROFICIENCY

| First Official Language | | | | |
|---|---|---|---|---|
| Proficiency Level | Speaking Points | Reading Points | Writing Points | Listening Points |
| Fluent | 6 | 6 | 6 | 6 |
| High | 5 | 5 | 5 | 5 |
| Moderate | 4 | 4 | 4 | 4 |
| Second Official Language | | | | |
| Proficiency Level | Speaking Points | Reading Points | Writing Points | Listening Points |
| Moderate | 1 | 1 | 1 | 1 |
| Basic | 0 | 0 | 0 | 0 |

To demonstrate your proficiency in French you must take the Test d'évaluation de français (TEF) (www.francais.cci-paris-idf.fr). In case you choose to take the TEF, you will have to submit to CIC the results of the following TEF tests: compréhension écrite, compréhension orale, expression écrite, and expression orale.

You will need to include the test results in your application. For skilled worker applications you must take the general test. Other forms of evidence will not be accepted. The results of the test must have been obtained within the last two years.

As you are unable to submit your application without the results of your language test, it is a good idea to do the test well in advance. This will also give you time to take the test again, in case you don't achieve a high enough score the first time.

It is your responsibility to make arrangements for taking the test and paying the applicable fees.

## 1.2  Age

The age criterion can bring you a maximum of 12 points. As can be seen in Table 2, Canada is looking for younger immigrants who can be economic contributors for a longer period of time. The points allocated for age shifts to a maximum of 12. In addition, the points favour younger applicants. Applicants aged 18 to 36 are able to score a maximum of 12 points. Applicants older than the age of 36 lose a point per year until age 46 after which they score zero points for age.

### Table 2
### FEDERAL SKILLED WORKER POINTS SYSTEM FOR AGE

| Age | Points Granted |
|---|---:|
| 17 or younger | 0 |
| 18 to 35 | 12 |
| 36 | 11 |
| 37 | 10 |
| 38 | 9 |
| 39 | 8 |
| 40 | 7 |
| 41 | 6 |
| 42 | 5 |
| 43 | 4 |
| 44 | 3 |
| 45 | 2 |
| 46 | 1 |
| 47 or older | 0 |

## 1.3  Education

Your education can bring you anywhere between 5 to 25 points based on your diplomas or degrees and years of study. Your studies must be full time (i.e., at least 15 hours per week during the academic year), or full-time equivalent (i.e., the same number of hours required for full-time studies, but on a part-time or intensive/accelerated basis). Table 3 shows the points awarded for educational qualifications.

## Table 3
## FEDERAL SKILLED WORKER POINTS SYSTEM
## FOR EDUCATION

| Education | Points Granted |
|---|---|
| High school diploma. | 5 |
| One-year postsecondary program credential. | 15 |
| Two-year postsecondary program credential. | 19 |
| Three-year postsecondary program credential. | 21 |
| Two or more postsecondary program credentials, one of which must be three years or longer. | 22 |
| University credential at the Master's level or an entry to practice professional degree (e.g., physician, lawyer, or accountant). | 23 |
| PhD or university credential at the doctoral level. | 25 |

All skilled worker applicants will now have to have their educational qualifications evaluated by an independent credential evaluation service. There is a list of credential assessment organizations designated by the Minister of Immigration (www.cic.gc.ca/english/immigrate/skilled/assessment.asp).

As of late 2011, the government announced its intention to accept international PhD students as permanent residents through the Federal Skilled Worker Program. To be eligible, you must have completed at least two years of study toward the attainment of a PhD degree and remain in good academic standing at a provincially recognized postsecondary educational institution in Canada.

If you have recently graduated from a Canadian PhD program, you will also be eligible to apply, provided you do so within 12 months of graduation. As of May 1, 2014, through to the end of year, Citizenship and Immigration Canada (CIC) will accept 500 applicants only under the PhD steam, until the introduction of the new Express Entry program (see Chapter 12).

## 1.4 Work experience

For work experience, you can earn between 9 and 15 points, provided that the experience was accumulated within the last ten years (see Table 4).

## Table 4
## FEDERAL SKILLED WORKER POINTS SYSTEM
## FOR WORK EXPERIENCE

| Years of Work Experience | Points Granted |
|---|---|
| 1 | 9 |
| 2-3 | 11 |
| 4-5 | 13 |
| 6+ | 15 |

Work experience only applies if it coincides with an occupation deemed eligible by Citizenship and Immigration Canada (CIC). The list of eligible occupations has recently been announced and can be found on CIC's website (www.cic.gc.ca/english/immigrate/skilled/apply-who-instructions.asp).

For an eligible occupation, you must demonstrate that you meet the National Occupational Classification (NOC) description for that occupation (www.esdc.gc.ca/eng/jobs/lmi/noc/index.shtml). Only occupations under NOC classifications at level O, A, or B are eligible for consideration under the skilled worker category.

For professions or trades who require licensing or trade certification, you will only be able to obtain this once you are in Canada. For example, doctors or electricians who get their immigration to Canada approved based on their profession being on the "list" will land here with only the "potential" to practise in those fields as they will have to undergo examinations, re-licensing, and more to practise those professions in Canada.

As has been the case in the past, there is a cap on the number of immigrants allowed in total as well as a cap for each occupation. You need to check whether the cap has been reached in a specific occupation or if the total number of applications has been received. The most recent list of occupations for the skilled workers' program was recently introduced on May 1, 2014, and was increased to 50 occupations (www.cic.gc.ca/english/immigrate/skilled/apply-who-instructions.asp?expand=jobs#jobs).

## 1.5 Adaptability

You can earn extra points for adaptability based on the information in Table 5.

## Table 5
## FEDERAL SKILLED WORKER POINTS SYSTEM
## FOR ADAPTABILITY

| Adaptability Requirements | Points Granted |
|---|---|
| You, as the principal applicant, have a minimum of one year legal work experience in Canada. | 10 |
| You have arranged employment in Canada. | 5 |
| You have, or your spouse or common-law partner has, completed a minimum of two years' study at a post-secondary institution in Canada, with a valid study permit (even if you do not have a degree from the institution). | 5 |
| Your spouse or common-law partner has one year of legal work experience in Canada. | 5 |
| You have, or your spouse or common-law partner has, a close relative in Canada who is 18 years of age or older. | 5 |
| Your spouse or common-law partner has basic language proficiency (CLB/NCLC 4). | 5 |

## 1.6 Arranged employment

In order to satisfy the arranged employment criteria you will need to apply to Service Canada for a permanent Labour Market Impact Assessment (LMIA) with a specific employer. This permanent LMIA will entitle you to apply for both a work permit and permanent residence and will give you 10 points on your skilled worker application.

## 1.7 Other factors

Apart from the six selection factors, you and your dependants will also have to undergo a medical exam as well as a criminal record check (see Chapter 3 for important details).

Unless you have a permanent Labour Market Impact Assessment (LMIA) or valid work permit in Canada, you will have to show proof that you have the necessary funds to support yourself and your family. The settlement funds that you need depend on the size of your family, as shown in Table 6 (note that these figures may be adjusted by CIC from time to time). Table 6 includes all totals in Canadian funds.

## Table 6
## MINIMUM FUNDS REQUIRED TO SUPPORT YOU
## AND YOUR FAMILY

| Family Members | Minimum Funds Required |
|---|---|
| 1 | $11,115 |
| 2 | $13,837 |
| 3 | $17,011 |
| 5 | $20,654 |
| 5 | $23,425 |
| 6 | $26,419 |
| 7+ | $29,414 |

# 2. The Application Process for Federal Skilled Workers

The steps of the application process are similar for most immigration classes: download the forms, complete them, pay the fees, and mail the application (see Chapter 3, section **4.** for general information about the process).

The forms can be downloaded from the Citizenship and Immigration Canada (CIC) website (www.cic.gc.ca/english/information/applications/skilled.asp). Do not panic if you made any mistakes when filling in your information because you can download the forms as many times as you wish, for no charge.

You need to download the following forms except those that do not apply to you (e.g., if you do not have any dependants joining you, you can skip steps 2, 6, and possibly 7):

1. Generic Application Form for Canada (IMM 0008)

2. Additional Dependants/Declaration (IMM 0008DEP)

3. Schedule A — Background/Declaration (IMM 5669)

4. Schedule 3: Economic Classes (IMM 0008 SCHEDULE 3)

5. Additional Family Information (IMM 5406)

6. Separation Declaration for Minors Travelling to Canada (IMM 5604)

7. Statutory Declaration of Common-law Union (IMM 5409)

8. Fee Payment Form — Application for Permanent Residence (IMM 5620)

9. Use of a Representative (IMM 5476)

If the application is not complete, it will be returned to you. As mentioned in Chapter 3, do not fill in any misleading or inaccurate information as that may result in your becoming inadmissible to Canada.

As of August 1, 2014, you may only include your dependants age 18 or younger in the application. Any dependant older than the age of 18 will not be included in your permanent resident application. This also applies to your children attending university or college; if they are older than 18 years of age, they will need to qualify on their own.

You will find instructions on how to pay the fees in the guide that comes with the application package. You will have to complete the Fee Payment Form — Application for Permanent Residence (IMM 5620) and include it with your application and provide the fees in Canadian funds by credit card, or certified cheque, bank draft, or money order made payable to the "Receiver General for Canada."

You will have to pay a processing fee for you and your spouse ($550 each) as well as your dependants aged 18 or younger ($150 each). These fees are refundable if your application is found to be ineligible. (All prices were current at the time of this book's publication.) Be sure to include the correct application fees for you and your dependants. If you fail to include the correct fee payment, your application will be considered incomplete and returned to you.

For skilled worker applications, mail your application and fees to the following address:

Centralized Intake Office
PO Box 7500
Sydney, Nova Scotia
Canada
B1P 0A9

If you are a skilled worker applicant with arranged employment, mail your application to the following address:

Centralized Intake Office
PO Box 8500
Sydney, Nova Scotia
Canada
B1P 0C4

You will find more information about the application guide on CIC's website (www.cic.gc.ca/english/information/applications/guides/EG7TOC.asp).

If your application is approved, you will also have to pay a Right of Permanent Residence fee ($490), which is refundable if you withdraw your application, or you do not use your visa before its expiration date. You can pay your Right of Permanent Residence fee at any time throughout the application process. Paying this fee at the time you submit your application may speed up the application process by several weeks.

See Chapter 3 for additional details regarding avoiding misrepresentation, reporting any change of circumstances, and the process for becoming a permanent resident.

# 6
# Business Immigration

Immigrant entrepreneurs have created some of the most successful and sustainable businesses in the world. For example, Silicon Valley in the United States has more than 60 percent of patents registered to immigrants! Experienced business people are a valuable asset to the Canadian economy, which is why Citizenship and Immigration Canada (CIC) began a Business Immigration Program to target immigrants who wish to own and manage businesses in Canada.

## 1. Investor and Entrepreneur Programs Are Terminated

You cannot presently immigrate under the Federal immigration program as an investor or entrepreneur as this program has been terminated. Under this program, there were three business classes which a prospective immigrant could apply: investors, entrepreneurs and self-employed persons. For now, only the Self-Employed Class is open for applications. The Minister of Immigration recently stated that both the investor and entrepreneur programs are expected to continue, but with revisions to the criteria. These new business programs will likely be introduced in early 2015.

The Entrepreneur Class was originally created to attract experienced businesspersons to establish and operate businesses in Canada that would contribute to the economy and create jobs. In recent years, application intake was declining, and processing times were taking six to eight years. Citizenship and Immigration Canada (CIC) is currently reviewing the program and considering new criteria.

> **Note:** Some provinces have an entrepreneur category in their Provincial Nominee Programs (PNPs), so all hope is not lost if you want to come to British Columbia, for example, as an entrepreneur. You will need to apply through the PNP program (see Chapter 7 for more information).

## 2. Start-up Visa Program

The former Immigration Minister, Jason Kenney, stated that he wanted the next Sun Microsystems or Apple to be created right here in Canada! On April 1, 2013, he introduced the first of its kind, the Start-up Visa.

"Our new Start-up Visa will help make Canada the destination of choice for the world's best and brightest to launch their companies," said Kenney. "Recruiting dynamic entrepreneurs from around the world will help Canada remain competitive in the global economy."[1]

The Start-up Visa program links immigrant entrepreneurs with private-sector organizations in Canada that have experience working with start-ups and who can provide essential resources. The program is part of a series of transformational changes to Canada's immigration system that makes it more focused on Canada's economic needs.

The Minister expects the application process to take less than six months and has set aside 2,750 visas a year for the next five years of the program, but expects interest will be slow to start and he wouldn't be surprised if just a few hundred apply in the program's early years.

---

1 "Immigration Canada to Lure Foreign Entrepreneurs with Prize of Permanent Residency," Nicholas Keung, thestar.com, accessed November 2014. http://www.thestar.com/news/canada/ 2013/01/24/immigration_canada_to_lure_foreign_entrepreneurs_with_prize_of_permanent_ residency.html

"We see the bright, young, international tech developers in the US who are stuck on temporary visas as an immediate market, if you will, for this program," Kenney said[2].

Applicants will require the support of a Canadian angel investor group or venture capital fund before they are able to apply for the Start-up Visa. Initial active partners in the program include the Canadian Venture Capital and Private Equity Association (CVCA), and National Angel Capital Organization (NACO). Citizenship and Immigration Canada (CIC) is also working with the Canadian Association of Business Incubation (CABI), and on October 26, 2013, introduced the business incubator stream as part of the Start-up Visa program. These approved industry partners will work with CIC to recommend suitable applicants for the Start-up Visa program. Expert peer-review panels will be established to assist visa officers in assessing applications for the new Start-up Visa.

This program is the first of its kind in the world in that it grants immediate permanent residence for the applicants selected. Many countries have business immigration programs that are generally conditional on the applicant either making an investment or establishing a business. The government acknowledges that not all start-up businesses will succeed, but is counting on the partnership with private-sector business organizations to enhance an applicant's likelihood of success. This new Start-up Visa program seeks to recruit innovative immigrant entrepreneurs who will create new jobs and spur economic growth in Canada.

In order to apply, applicants will first need the support of one of the approved industry financial organizations (i.e., CVCA, NACO, or CABI) who will provide the applicants with both the financial resources to back their proposed venture as well as ongoing business support. In addition to being matched with an approved industry sector partner, applicants must also meet the following basic criteria:

- Language proficiency at an intermediate language benchmark of 5.

- At least one year of postsecondary education.

Canada's Economic Action Plan 2012 highlighted the commitment to supporting innovators, entrepreneurs, and world-class

---

2 "Canada Looks to Poach Entrepreneurial Immigrants from Silicon Valley," Tobi Cohen, Canada.com, accessed November 2014. http://o.canada.com/news/national/revamped-immigrant-entrepreneur-visa-set-to-go-april-1

researchers. The government of Canada declared its intention to establish a fast and flexible economic immigration system to facilitate addressing the ongoing and emerging needs of the Canadian economy. This new program is a pilot project as defined in the ministerial instructions. It has the following objectives:

- Test the potential for increased economic benefit to Canada by linking foreign entrepreneurs with Canadian private sector partners that have experience and expertise dealing with start-up businesses.

- Enable immigrant entrepreneurs to create jobs in Canada and build innovative companies that can compete on a global scale.

- Provide private sector firms with access to a broader range of entrepreneurs including the best and the brightest minds from around the world.

The new start-up business class is part of the overall business immigration program and is designed to complement rather than supplement existing business immigration program criteria.

For applicants to be eligible as in the start-up business class visa applicant, they must obtain a Commitment Certificate issued by a designated partner. The start-up business class is a prescribed class of applicants who are eligible to become permanent residents based on their ability to demonstrate that they can be economically established in Canada as an innovative businessperson. The following objectives have been set for applicants for permanent residents under the start-up business class:

- No more than 2,750 applications per year.

- No more than five persons per business proposal.

- Only persons who intend to reside in a province or territory other than Quebec.

- Persons who have the support of a Canadian business entity, in the form of a Commitment Certificate.

- Persons who meet or exceed the minimum language proficiency threshold in English or French for each of the four language skill areas.

- Persons who have completed at least one year of postsecondary education.

- Persons who have sufficient funds to economically establish themselves in Canada.

## 2.1 The application process for the Start-up Visa

At the time you submit your application, you will need to send your supporting documentation together with the application forms. You can obtain an application kit from the website of Citizenship and Immigration Canada (CIC), complete the forms, attach the supporting documents, pay the fees, and submit your application.

You will find the following forms on the Government of Canada's website (Quebec Selected Business Class Applicants: www. cic.gc.ca/english/information/applications/business.asp — Skilled Worker Class: www.cic.gc.ca/english/information/applications/ skilled.asp):

1. Document Checklist (IMM 5722)

2. Generic Application Form for Canada (IMM 0008)

3. Additional Dependants/Declaration (IMM 0008DEP)

4. Schedule A — Background/Declaration (IMM 5669)

5. Schedule 13 — Business Immigration Programs — Start-up Business Class (IMM 0008 SCHEDULE 13)

6. Additional Family Information (IMM 5406)

7. Statutory Declaration of Common-law Union (IMM 5409)

8. Declaration from Non-Accompanying Parent/Guardian for Minors Immigrating to Canada (IMM 5604)

9. Supplementary Information — Your Travels (IMM 5562)

10. Fee Payment Form — Application for Permanent Residence (IMM 5620)

11. Use of a Representative (IMM 5476)

If the application is not complete, it will be returned to you. As mentioned in Chapter 3, do not fill in any misleading or inaccurate information as that may result in your becoming inadmissible to Canada.

You will find instructions on how to pay the fees in the guide that comes with the application package. You will have to complete the Fee Payment Form — Application for Permanent Residence (IMM 5620) and include it with your application and provide the fees in Canadian funds by credit card, or certified cheque, bank draft, or money order made payable to the "Receiver General for Canada."

You will have to pay a processing fee for you, as the principal applicant ($1,050) and your spouse ($550 each) as well as your dependants aged 18 or younger ($150). These fees are refundable if your application is found to be ineligible. Be sure to include the correct application fees for you and your dependants. If you fail to include the correct fee payment, your application will be considered incomplete and returned to you.

Mail your application and fees to the following address:

Centralized Intake Office
PO Box 8500
Sydney, Nova Scotia
Canada
B1P 0C9

If your application is approved, you will also have to pay a Right of Permanent Residence Fee for each adult applicant ($490), which is also refundable in case you withdraw your application, or you do not use your visa before its expiration date. You can pay your Right of Permanent Residence fee at any time throughout the application process. Paying this fee at the time you submit your application may speed up the application process by several weeks.

See Chapter 3 for additional details regarding avoiding misrepresentation, reporting any change of circumstances, and the process for becoming a permanent resident.

## 3. Self-employed Persons

To immigrate as a self-employed person, you have to have the intention and ability to become self-employed in Canada. This category is very specifically defined to persons who create their own employment through cultural, athletic, or farming activities. You do not need to have owned a business, but you do need to demonstrate that you have either relevant, world-class experience that could significantly contribute to the cultural or athletic life in Canada, or experience in farm management, with the intention to purchase and manage a farm in Canada.

While there is no regulated minimum net worth requirement, you will have to satisfy a visa officer that you have sufficient funds to settle in Canada with your dependants, and to finance the economic activities on which your selection was based.

You need to have at least two years of experience in the fields mentioned above, accumulated in the five years before applying for permanent residence. The two years can be consecutive, or divided into two one-year periods. You must also be able to demonstrate that you have earned enough income to support you and all of your dependants as a result of your self-employed activities. Other sources of income will not be taken into consideration for the purposes of determining whether you meet the self-employed criteria.

## 3.1 Eligibility and the point system for self-employed persons

There is a points calculation for the self-employed category. A successful applicant needs a minimum point score of 35 points considering an applicant's education, experience, age, language proficiency, and adaptability to Canada. An applicant's education is assessed as set out in Table 7.

In order to obtain the points for education, it will be necessary to provide a copy of your education credential (along with the translations of English or French, if necessary) demonstrating that you have completed the education that you are claiming.

Self-employed business experience will only be considered in the immediate five years preceding the date of you application with points being awarded as shown in Table 8.

Applicants must provide objective proof of their experience such as tax returns, bank statements, financial records, and confirmation from the accountant's records.

The maximum points for age are 10 with a decrease of 2 points per year beyond the range of 21 to 49 years.

Points are awarded proficiency in both English or French with 16 possible points for your first official language and a further 8 possible points for your second official language for a total maximum points score of 24 points. See Table 9.

You may earn 6 points under the adaptability factor as shown in Table 10.

### Table 7
## SELF-EMPLOYED PERSONS POINTS SYSTEM FOR EDUCATION

| Education | Maximum 25 |
|---|---|
| Doctorate or Master's Degree plus 17 years of full-time or full-time equivalent studies. | 25 |
| Three-year Trade Certificate, Bachelor of Law, or Medical Degree plus 15 years full-time or full-time equivalent studies. | 22 |
| Bachelor's Degree or two-year Trade Certificate plus 14 years full-time or full-time equivalent studies. | 20 |
| Bachelor's Degree or one-year Trade Certificate plus 13 years full-time or full-time equivalent studies. | 15 |
| One year postsecondary plus 12 years full-time or full-time equivalent studies. | 12 |
| Secondary school education | 5 |

### Table 8
## SELF-EMPLOYED PERSONS POINTS SYSTEM FOR EXPERIENCE

| Relevant Experience | Maximum 35 |
|---|---|
| Five years' relevant experience. | 35 |
| Four years' relevant experience. | 30 |
| Three years' relevant experience. | 25 |
| Two years' relevant experience. | 20 |

## Table 9
## SELF-EMPLOYED PERSONS POINTS SYSTEM
## FOR LANGUAGE

| Official Language | 1st Language | 2nd Language |
|---|---|---|
| High proficiency | 16 | 8 |
| Moderate proficiency | 8 | 8 |
| Basic proficiency | 2 | 2 |
| No proficiency | 0 | 0 |

## Table 10
## SELF-EMPLOYED PERSONS POINTS SYSTEM
## FOR ADAPTABILITY

| Adaptability | Maximum 6 |
|---|---|
| Spouse's or common-law partner's education. | 3-5 |
| Minimum one year's full-time authorized work in Canada. | 5 |
| Minimum two years' full-time postsecondary studies in Canada. | 5 |
| Family members in Canada. | 5 |

Clearly, the most significant factor in the self-employed category is experience. Five years of relevant self-employed work experience scores 35 points, which is the pass mark for this category.

Just like for the other immigration categories, you and your dependants will have to undergo medical exams and criminal and security checks, and also demonstrate that you have sufficient funds to support yourselves in Canada.

## 3.2 The application process for self-employed persons

At the time you submit your application, you will need to send your supporting documentation together with the application forms. The supporting documentation needs to demonstrate that you have been able to support yourself and your family as a result of your self-employed activities for at least two of the past five years. The application procedure is a standard one: obtain an application kit from the website of Citizenship and Immigration Canada (CIC), complete the forms, attach the supporting documents, pay the fees, and submit your application. The forms you will need are as follows (http://www.cic.gc.ca/english/information/applications/business.asp):

1. Generic Application Form for Canada (IMM 0008)

2. Schedule A: Background/Declaration (IMM 5669)

3. Additional Family Information (IMM 5406)

4. Schedule 6: Business Immigrants — Investors and Entrepreneurs (IMM 0008 SCHEDULE 6)

5. Fee Payment Form — Application for Permanent Residence (IMM 5620)

6. Use of a Representative (IMM 5476)

If the application is not complete, it will be returned to you. As mentioned in Chapter 3, do not fill in any misleading or inaccurate information as that may result in your becoming inadmissible to Canada.

You will find instructions on how to pay the fees in the guide that comes with the application package. You will have to complete the Fee Payment Form — Application for Permanent Residence (IMM 5620) and include it with your application and provide the fees in Canadian funds by credit card, or certified cheque, bank draft, or money order made payable to the "Receiver General for Canada."

You will have to pay a processing fee for yourself as the principal applicant ($1,050) and your spouse ($550 each) as well as your dependants aged 18 or younger ($150 each). These fees are refundable if your application is found to be ineligible. Be sure to include the correct application fees for you and your dependants. If you fail to include the correct fee payment, your application will be considered incomplete and returned to you.

For self-employed applications, mail your application and fees to the following address:

Centralized Intake Office
PO Box 7200
Sydney, Nova Scotia

Canada
B1P 0E9

If your application is approved, you will also have to pay a Right of Permanent Residence Fee for you and your spouse ($490 each), which is also refundable in case you withdraw your application, or you do not use your visa before its expiration date. You can pay your Right of Permanent Residence fee at any time throughout the application process. Paying this fee at the time you submit your application may speed up the application process by several weeks.

See Chapter 3 for additional details regarding avoiding misrepresentation, reporting any change of circumstances, and the process for becoming a permanent resident.

# 7
# Provincial Nominee Program

Canada's fastest-growing immigration program is actually several programs across Canada, known as the Provincial Nominee Programs (PNPs). They are employer-driven immigration programs that give provinces and territories an active role in immigrant selection to meet specific local labour market needs, although each province and territory is only allowed a certain number annually. About 44,500 to 47,000 people are expected to immigrate to Canada under PNPs in 2014, including the nominees themselves, their spouses, and their dependants.

PNPs are an increasingly attractive option for people who want to immigrate to Canada, given the increasing restrictions in other immigration categories. As an immigrant, you can obtain a direct sponsorship or nomination from an employer, municipality, province, or territory to come to Canada, most commonly in the form of an employment offer. Employers facing labour shortages consider the program a good option for them to fill their staffing needs.

PNPs vary across the country, but virtually all provinces and territories have a program. In all PNPs, you can immigrate as a skilled worker, and with some programs you can even be nominated as a semiskilled worker, student, graduate student, or businessperson, which is an alternative to the now terminated Federal Investor and Entrepreneur programs.

Of course, you must meet the basic criteria of the specific provincial or territorial program as well as Canada immigration requirements including medical exams, and criminal and security checks (see Chapter 3).

> **Note:** As of January 1, 2015, the program will also be included in the new Express Entry program (see Chapter 12).

## 1.  Choose a Province or Territory

Your first step is to identify which province or territory you want to live in and then seek employment. Every province and territory have their own rules for this program, tailored to their own special requirements. Currently, all provinces and territories, with the exception of Quebec and Nunavut, have Provincial Nominee Programs (PNPs). You will find a list of links for the PNP of each province in the Resources section at the end of this book.

In order to be nominated, you have to show that you have the skills, experience, and education necessary to make an immediate contribution to the economy of the province or territory that nominates you. You must also demonstrate that you have the intention to settle permanently in that province or territory.

## 2.  Get a Job Offer

The most common way to immigrate under a Provincial Nominee Program (PNP) is to secure an employment offer from a company in that province or territory. Make sure that your employer meets any necessary employer criteria for the program you are considering.

This is perhaps easier said than done. How exactly does one get a job in Canada if you're still living overseas? You can apply online for many jobs in Canada. However, similar to immigrants who have already landed here, finding a job in Canada comes with many barriers for newcomers (See Chapter 16). There are many industries in Canada with labour shortages so you may have some luck depending on your field and if you're willing to move to smaller towns or outlying regions.

Some people who come here as temporary workers may find their employer is willing to offer them full-time employment. In that case, they can then apply under the PNP, although there may be some restrictions on the type of eligible employment.

Others may come to Canada as visitors and spend their time looking for work. If they are lucky enough to get a job offer, the person and employer can do the paperwork required to nominate the person. Employers often don't have the time or the know-how to do the paperwork, but you can take the initiative and tell the employer that you would be willing to do the paperwork if you are given a job. As a visitor, you must then return to your home country to apply via the program. If the employer is willing, you can also seek a temporary worker visa first to get you here sooner. You can then apply for permanent residence while you are already working in Canada.

## 3. Other PNP Options

In addition to coming through the Provincial Nominee Program (PNP) as a skilled worker, you may also apply as a business applicant, farmer, student, or semiskilled worker depending on the province or territory. Some provinces and territories (i.e., British Columbia, Saskatchewan, Manitoba, Ontario, Newfoundland and Labrador, Prince Edward Island, Northwest Territories, and Yukon) have a business or investment side to their PNPs. So while you are no longer able to apply as an investor or entrepreneur under the federal Business Immigration Program, you might be able to get here directly to one of these provinces or territories looking for entrepreneurs to add to their economy.

In addition to business programs, some provinces have options tailored specifically to their economies; for example, Alberta's and Saskatchewan's PNP allows immigrants who want to come to the province and purchase or start a farming business. Alberta's PNP also has a special focus on semiskilled workers (e.g., hospitality workers, manufacturing, long-haul trucking, and food services), tradespersons, and engineers. Saskatchewan's semiskilled program focuses on health care, hospitality, and long-haul trucking industries.

The Northwest Territories and Yukon are open to "critical impact workers" in sectors such as hospitality and service. British

Columbia allows you to apply for permanent residence as a semi-skilled worker after working in the province for nine months, but again these are in very specific industry sectors.

Most PNPs accept applications from international student graduates, particularly in the health fields. Several provinces such as Saskatchewan, Manitoba, Newfoundland and Labrador, Nova Scotia, and Prince Edward Island also have a "family connections" option, which may allow you to immigrate if you have a close family connection in the province.

Ultimately, each province and territory have a program that best suits their needs, which may also change periodically, so research all the websites listed in the Resources at the end of this book. You need to become familiar with the various PNP options that exist in the province or territory in which you intend to reside. You may find the right fit for you in a province you had never even considered before.

## 4. The Application Process

The Provincial Nominee Program (PNP) process has two steps: First, applying to the province or territory of your choice; and second applying to the Citizenship and Immigration Canada (CIC). You will need to submit your PNP application to the provincial or territorial office with the appropriate PNP and CIC immigration forms together with the PNP processing fees. When your application is approved, you will receive a nomination certificate from that province or territory.

Once you have been nominated, you may apply to CIC for permanent residence. You may have already prepared the application forms at the outset of applying to the PNP office; each province and territory has a different process and requirements. If not, you need to download and print the application package and complete your application. You'll need the following forms (http://www.cic.gc.ca/english/information/applications/prov-apply-application.asp):

1. Generic Application Form for Canada (IMM 0008)

2. Schedule A: Background/Declaration (IMM 5669)

3. Schedule 4: Economic Classes: Provincial Nominees (IMM 0008 SCHEDULE 4)

4. Additional Family Information (IMM 5406)

5. Use of a Representative (IMM 5476)

6. Document Checklist (IMM 5690)

7. Fee Payment Form — Application for Permanent Residence (IMM 5620)

You must submit your application to the Centralized Intake Office (CIO) in Sydney, Nova Scotia at the following address:

Citizenship and Immigration
Centralized Intake Office
Provincial Nominee Program
PO Box 1450
Sydney, Nova Scotia
Canada
B1P 6K5

If the CIO determines that your application is complete, it will be sent to the appropriate CIC processing office. The processing office will contact you for further documentation once it is ready to process your application.

If your application does not include all of the documents and forms set out in the Document Checklist (IMM 5690), CIC will return it to you. Do not provide documents that are not listed in the checklist.

The procedure for PNP applications may vary slightly from one visa office to another. You will have to determine which visa office will process your application and then download the instructions of that particular office from CIC's website. The instructions will cover different topics, such as paying your fees, obtaining your police certificate, and undergoing the medical exam. See Chapter 3 for additional details regarding avoiding misrepresentation, reporting any change of circumstances, and the process for becoming a permanent resident.

You have to pay PNP fees when you apply to the province or territory and then CIC fees when you make the permanent residence application. You will find instructions on how to pay the fees in the guide that comes with the application package.

You will have to pay a processing fee for you and your spouse ($550 each) as well as your dependants aged 18 or younger ($150 each). These fees are refundable if your application is found to be ineligible. Be sure to include the correct application fees for you and your dependants. If you fail to include the correct fee payment, your application will be considered incomplete and returned to you.

If your application is approved, you and your spouse will also have to pay a Right of Permanent Residence Fee ($490 each), which is also refundable in case you withdraw your application, or you do not use your visa before its expiration date. You can pay your Right of Permanent Residence fee at any time throughout the application process. Paying this fee at the time you submit your application may speed up the application process by several weeks.

You will have to prove that you have enough funds to support yourself and your dependants after you arrive in Canada. The funds you need depend on the size of your family, as shown in Table 11 (note all funds are in Canadian dollars):

### Table 11
### PNP PROGRAM MINIMUM FUNDS REQUIRED TO SUPPORT YOURSELF AND YOUR FAMILY*

| Family Members | Minimum Sum Required |
|---|---|
| 1 | $11,824 |
| 2 | $14,720 |
| 3 | $18,097 |
| 4 | $21,971 |
| 5 | $24,920 |
| 6 | $28,105 |
| 7+ | $31,291 |

*Note: These figures change every year so be sure to check CIC's website to ensure that you can demonstrate that you have sufficient financial resources for your family to settle in Canada.

# 8
# Family Class: Spouses and Children

While some people make the immigration journey alone, most immigrants want to bring their loved ones with them, whether immediately or later on after they've settled. As a permanent resident or Canadian citizen, you can sponsor certain family members to join you in Canada, such as spouses, natural or adopted children, parents, and grandparents, and whether they are living outside or inside Canada.

This chapter will focus on bringing your immediate family, such as your spouse or partner, and your children, while Chapter 9 will look at sponsoring parents, grandparents, adopted children, and other eligible relatives.

Close family members (and their dependants) of Canadian citizens or permanent residents who live in countries that are undergoing a serious major crisis (e.g., certain Middle Eastern countries) will be given priority by the visa offices when processing the sponsorship applications. This is valid even for family members who have already applied as refugees; they can apply under the Family Class as well.

> **Note:** As of August 1, 2014, the age of a dependant that you can sponsor has decreased from younger than the age of 22 to younger than the age of 19. This means only dependant children 18 years of age or younger can be sponsored. Dependant children who are attending university are no longer eligible to be sponsored.

# 1. Bringing Your Immediate Family

If you are presently considering immigrating to Canada, but have not started the application process yet, you should know that it may be easier to bring your family with you as dependants under your own application, rather than have them reunite with you later. When you apply for permanent residence under other classes such as the Federal Skilled Worker or the Self-employed categories, you can bring your spouse or partner and children with you when you immigrate.

However, if you decide to immigrate alone, but plan to bring your immediate family over later under the Family Class category, make sure to mention them on your application. This is very important, as failure to do so may result in their being ineligible for a Family Class visa later, and you could find yourself permanently separated from your loved ones if you choose to stay in Canada.

If you are already a Canadian citizen or permanent resident and are planning to sponsor, for example, a new spouse that you met and married overseas, you need to brace yourself because you are looking at a wait period of between 6 to 18 months, and sometimes longer, depending on several factors.

## 1.1 Requirements and responsibilities

If you are older than 18 years of age, you can apply to sponsor your spouse or partner and dependant children (up to 18 years of age) to join you in Canada. Sponsorship is a major, long-term commitment that cannot be taken back after the permanent residence visa is issued to your sponsored family member. Before you start the application process, you need to be aware of the responsibilities that await you as a sponsor.

You will need to make a written commitment called a Sponsorship Agreement, which is a Citizenship and Immigration Canada

(CIC) document signed by yourself and the sponsored person, in which you promise to financially support him or her for a certain period after he or she becomes a permanent resident. This means that you will be required to show evidence that your income is sufficient to carry out this promise.

In the case of a spouse or partner, the minimum period for which you have to offer support is three years after he or she is granted permanent residence. The sponsored spouse or partner also commits to making all the necessary efforts to support himself or herself. In the case of a child, the minimum period of support is ten years, or until the child turns 25, whichever happens first.

Keep in mind that you cannot cancel this agreement once the visa has been granted. Breaking up, moving, having a major disagreement, or no longer being able to afford to support the sponsored person do not constitute reasons for cancelling the sponsorship.

Unfortunately, there have been documented cases in recent years of marriage fraud, where unsuspecting Canadians or permanent residents fall in love with someone who lives overseas, marry and sponsor them to Canada (or alternatively are set up in an arranged marriage and sponsor them to Canada), only to find themselves dumped once their new spouse lands in Canada. The real tragedy is that the sponsors are still financially responsible for their spouses, as mentioned above.

In 2010, CIC underwent a consultation process to improve the system in order to investigate the issue of marriage fraud further, and has instituted some new rules to help prevent such cases. One of these new rules is a five-year ban on future sponsorships for new immigrants where there is a marriage breakdown after arriving in Canada. These new rules affect any new spousal sponsorship immigrant who has arrived in Canada as well as those whose applications have been submitted after the new rules came into effect on March 2, 2012.

In addition, the Minister of Immigration has recently implemented a two-year conditional permanent resident visa for a sponsored spouse. This means that for newly sponsored spouses, they have to remain married to and live with their Canadian sponsors for a period of two years after arriving in Canada or they will lose their permanent residence status. There is an exemption to this provision for spouses who have been in marital relationships for three years prior to submitting their application or who have children together.

## 1.2 Possible impediments to becoming a sponsor

Certain factors can keep you from becoming a sponsor. You cannot sponsor your family members if the following applies:

- You have served or are serving a prison sentence.
- You are the subject of a removal order.
- You are an undischarged bankrupt (i.e., you have not been discharged from bankruptcy proceedings).
- You have missed payments on an immigration loan or support order (e.g., alimony).
- You have been convicted of a violent or sexual crime.
- You have received government assistance (except in cases of disability).
- You have broken the terms of a previous sponsorship agreement.

# 2. Sponsoring a Spouse

In order to sponsor a spouse, you have to be in a legally valid marriage or common-law relationship with the sponsored person, according to the laws of the country or territory where the marriage was officiated.

This includes same-sex marriages from territories or countries that legally recognize them, or recognized them at the time the marriage was officiated. Same-sex marriages performed in the following jurisdictions are recognized by Citizenship and Immigration Canada (CIC) for the purposes of a Family Class application:

- Argentina
- Belgium
- Brazil
- Canada
- Denmark

- France

- Iceland

- Luxembourg

- Mexico

- Netherlands

- Norway

- Portugal

- South Africa

- Spain

- Sweden

- United Kingdom

- Some states in the United States

- Uruguay.

Obviously, this list may change over time, as more and more countries consider legalizing same-sex marriages.

If the same-sex marriage was performed in Canada, it is considered valid if it was performed after the following dates in Table 12.

## Table 12
## DATES ENACTED FOR CANADIAN SAME-SEX MARRIAGE LAWS

| Province/Territory | Start Date |
|---|---|
| Ontario | June 10, 2003 |
| British Columbia | July 8, 2003 |
| Quebec | March 19, 2004 |
| Yukon | July 14, 2004 |
| Manitoba | September 16, 2004 |
| Nova Scotia | September 24, 2004 |
| Saskatchewan | November 5, 2004 |
| Newfoundland and Labrador | December 21, 2004 |
| New Brunswick | July 4, 2005 |
| All other provinces and territories | July 20, 2005 |

# 3. Common-law Partnerships

Common-law partnerships are established by living together in a conjugal relationship for an uninterrupted period of 12 months, but exceptions are made in case of short absences due to work or family related reasons. Common-law partners can be of the opposite or the same sex.

Citizenship and Immigration Canada (CIC) will require you to show evidence of your shared life. This means providing joint rental agreements, rental receipts, utility bills, documents for joint ownership of a home, banking and credit card records, receipts for joint purchases, and other similar documentation.

# 4. Conjugal Partnerships

The category of conjugal partnerships deals with those special situations in which partners in a committed relationship are unable to get married or live together due to circumstances that are beyond their control. Such circumstances can include the following:

- Immigration barriers.

- Marital status (one of the partners is married in a country where divorce is not an option).

- Sexual orientation (for countries where same-sex marriages are not acknowledged).

- Refusal of long-term stays in each other's countries.

Whatever the circumstances may be, you will have to share them with Citizenship and Immigration Canada (CIC) officers and prove that you had a very serious reason for not having lived together or gotten married.

The conjugal relationship has to be of at least one year in length and has to demonstrate a level of involvement similar to that of a marriage or common-law partnership. Not all star-crossed lover situations qualify you for the category of conjugal partners. For example, if you could have lived together or gotten married, but chose not to, or if you can't provide any evidence that a reason beyond your control prevented you from getting married or living together, then you are not eligible for this category.

Also, for those who are engaged to be married, you must wait until the marriage has taken place and then apply as a spouse or apply as a common-law partner, if you have lived together for more than 12 months.

The following are not eligible to sponsor a spouse under the Family Class:

- You are younger than 18.

- You are or your sponsor is involved in a marriage or common-law partnership with another person.

- Your spouse or common-law partner immigrated to Canada and, at the time he or she applied, you were not examined to see if you meet immigration requirements.

- Your partner is not yet free of a previous sponsorship agreement.

## 5. Children as Dependants

You can bring your dependant children to Canada under the Family Class category. You can sponsor your dependant minor children up to the age of 18 years of age. As of August 1, 2014, your children who are 19 years of age or older, regardless of whether they are attending school, must apply for immigration on their own merit.

## 6. The Application Process

You have the option to sponsor your spouse or partner and your dependant children (up to 18 years of age) at the same time, as long as you complete and mail their applications together.

You must get two application packages: one for sponsorship and one for permanent residence. You will apply as a sponsor, and your spouse or partner and any dependant children will apply for permanent residence. The sponsorship and permanent residence applications must be sent at the same time (www.cic.gc.ca/english/information/applications/fc.asp).

You'll need the following sponsorship forms:

1. Guide to Sponsorship (IMM 3900)

2. Document Checklist (IMM 5491)

3. Application to Sponsor, Sponsorship Agreement and Undertaking (IMM 1344)

4. Sponsorship Evaluation (IMM 5481)

5. Statutory Declaration of Common-Law Union (IMM 5409

6. Sponsor Questionnaire (IMM 5540)

7. Use of a Representative (IMM 5476)

You'll also need the following permanent resident immigration forms:

1. Sponsorship of a Spouse, Common-Law Partner, Conjugal Partner or Dependent Child Living Outside Canada (IMM 3999)

2. Generic Application Form for Canada (IMM 0008)

3. Additional Dependants/Declaration (IMM 008DEP)

4. Schedule A — Background/Declaration (IMM 5406)

5. Additional Family Information (IMM 5406)

6. Sponsored Spouse/Partner Questionnaire (IMM 5490)

7. Use of a Representative (IMM 5476)

You must submit your application to Mississauga, Ontario, at the Case Processing Centre (CPC):

CPC Mississauga
PO Box 3000, Station A
Mississauga, ON
L5A 4N6

Fill in the forms and attach all the required documentation. If any documents are missing, your waiting time may increase. As mentioned in Chapter 3, do not fill in any misleading or inaccurate information as that may result in your spouse, partner, or child becoming inadmissible to Canada.

Further, when you send the sponsorship application and the permanent residence application, you need to include the confirmation that you have completed the medical examination. If you don't include proof of your medical examination, your application will be returned to you. You can also send your criminal record checks as well although these can be provided at a later date if you don't have them at the outset of the application process. **Note:** Proof of your medical examination is a Citizenship and Immigration Canada (CIC) form that is in the application package that you take to the Designated Medical Practitioner (DMP) to complete and give to you to include in your application package. The actual medical results are sent by the DMP directly to CIC's medical branch and then transmitted to the visa officer. You must include proof that you have completed your medical examination in your application package at the outset or your application will be returned to you as incomplete.

## 6.1 Fees

The next steps are to pay the fees and mail your application. Online payment on the website of Citizenship and Immigration Canada (CIC) is preferred. When you pay online, remember to print the receipt of payment form because you will need to include that in your application. Read the instructions in the application package carefully, and double check your eligibility and that of the person you wish to sponsor, because the processing fees are not refundable.

You can also pay the fees at most banks, or, if you (the sponsor) live outside Canada, you can pay with an international money order or bank draft, in Canadian funds, made out to the "Receiver General of Canada." In the latter case, you need to write the name, complete address, and account number of the bank you are using on the back of the money order or bank draft.

The fees for the family class are the following:

- Principal applicant and spouse: $550 each.

- Dependant child of the principal applicant who is 18 or younger and not married or in a common-law partnership: $150 per dependant.

If the application is approved, you will also have to pay a Right of Permanent Residence Fee ($490 each), which is refundable in case you withdraw your application, or you do not use your visa before its expiration date. You can pay your Right of Permanent Residence fee at any time throughout the application process. Paying this fee at the time you submit your application may speed up the application process by several weeks.

Once your sponsorship is approved — you will be notified of this by the Case Processing Centre (CPC) — the application for permanent residence of your spouse, partner, or child will be processed. If you apply from outside Canada, CPC will send the application to the visa office responsible for your country.

See Chapter 3 for additional details regarding avoiding misrepresentation, reporting any change of circumstances, and the process for becoming a permanent resident.

# 7. Appealing the Decision

If you qualify as a sponsor, but the application of your family member is rejected, you may appeal to the Immigration and Appeal Division of the Immigration and Refugee Board.

If you are not approved as a sponsor, your relative may proceed with another immigration application, or apply to stay in Canada on humanitarian and compassionate grounds.

Some situations do not give you the right to an appeal, such as the following:

- Providing false or misleading information.

- Withdrawing or abandoning the sponsorship application.

- Failing to meet the eligibility criteria for spouses, partners, or dependant children.

- Existing serious criminal offence in the applicant's background.

- Security reasons such as human rights violations or involvement in organized crime.

See Chapter 13 for more information about appealing a decision.

# 9

# Family Class: Parents, Grandparents, Adopted Children, and Other Eligible Relatives

It is a common belief that bringing one's family to Canada is a very simple and fast procedure. Citizenship and Immigration Canada (CIC) gives spouses and children first priority for processing of these applications, but it has been far from the same story for the sponsorship of other relatives, such as parents, grandparents, adopted children, and other specific family relationships. The sponsorship of parents and grandparents has been a particularly popular program.

The Family Class category for these relatives has had one of the longest wait times, and requires applicants to submit substantial documentation. In recent years, the wait times for processing parent and grandparent sponsorship applications have become very long, with some families waiting close to a decade to be reunited! As a result, in November of 2011, the Minister of Immigration introduced a two-year hold on new parent and grandparent applications to reduce the backlog. Concurrent with the suspension of the program, a new parent and grandparent Super Visa was introduced to help alleviate this program suspension. (See more about this option later in section **3**.) On January 2, 2014, the Minister of Immigration reopened the parent and grandparent category accepting the first 5,000 applicants. The program is now closed until January 2, 2015.

# 1. Sponsorship Criteria

On May 10, 2013, the Minister of Immigration announced that the parent and grandparent family class sponsorship program would be reopening on January 2015. The Citizenship, Immigration and Multiculturalism Minister at the time, Jason Kenney, stated, "The Action Plan for Faster Family Reunification is on track to meet the goals of cutting in half the backlog and wait times in the Parent And Grandparent Program. It is very important that we continue to make progress and not return to the old broken system with wait times as long as a decade — that would be unfair to families."[1]

When this category was frozen there were approximately 165,000 applications pending for consideration and processing levels at that time were approximately 15,000 applications per year.

This second phase of the "Action Plan for Faster Family Reunification" features the following:

1. **Processing levels increase:** While Phase 1 of the program saw processing levels for parents and grandparents increase from 15,000 to 25,000 per year, in Phase 2 these levels will increase to 50,000 parents and grandparents per year for 2012 and 2013 with a further commitment that processing levels will remain high for parents and grandparents in 2014. The objective of these increased processing levels is to eliminate the outstanding backlog of applications. It is anticipated that as the backlog is eliminated, projected targets will stabilize to a higher standard annual level (more than 5,000 applications per year), but that the specified higher levels for 2014 will allow for flexibility in maintaining high targets to completely resolve the backlog of applications.

2. **The Super Visa is here to stay:** The Super Visa becomes a permanent program allowing applicants to obtain a ten-year multiple entry visa and remain in Canada for up to two years at a time. This program has been very successful

---

[1] "Action Plan for Faster Family Reunification on Track to Cut Backlog in Half," *The Weekly Voice,* accessed November 2014. http://www.weeklyvoice.com/new_immigrants_canada/action-plan-for-faster-family-reunification-on-track-to-cut-backlog-in-half/

in welcoming more than 15,000 parents and grandparents with Super Visas since its launch in December of 2011 and with an overall approval rate of 86 percent.

3. **Program criteria change:** The qualifying criteria for sponsors of parents and grandparents has changed increasing the necessary financial ability of sponsors in order to ensure they have the financial ability to provide for their sponsored family members for a longer period of time. The key changes to the program criteria are as follows:

  • Increase the minimum necessary income (MNI) for sponsoring parents and grandparents by 30 percent from current Low Income Cut Off (LICO) levels.

  • Lengthen the period necessary for demonstrating MNI from one year to three years.

  • Evidence of income will be confined to documents issued by Canada Revenue Agency (CRA).

  • Extend the sponsorship undertaking period from 10 years to 20 years.

  • Change the maximum age for accompanying dependants to 18 years in all application categories effective August 1, 2014.

## 2. Who You Can Sponsor

The restrictions on sponsoring parents and grandparents does not extend to the other eligible relatives under this category, so sponsoring an adopted child is still possible under the Family Class, as is a grandchild, sibling, nephew, or niece, but they must be orphaned, 18 or younger, and not married or involved in a common-law relationship.

If you do not have relatives who fall under the above-mentioned categories, you can sponsor a relative of any age and relationship, but only if you do not have any other relatives who are Canadian citizens or permanent residents, or any other relatives abroad who could be sponsored under the Family Class. You truly need to be completely alone in Canada and with no sponsor-able relatives overseas to be able to sponsor someone under this provision.

The eligibility of relatives to immigrate to Canada also depends on their medical, criminal, and background checks. They will be required to provide a police certificate from their home country. People with a criminal record and who may be a threat to Canada's security are not allowed to enter the country. Similarly, persons with serious medical conditions who will likely require significant medical treatment that imposes "an excessive demand on health care or social services" will not be eligible to immigrate.

Other relatives, such as brothers and sisters older than 18, or adult independent children (i.e., children 19 years of age or older regardless of whether they are in full-time attendance at a post-secondary institute, children who are married or in common-law partnerships), cannot be sponsored. However, if they apply to immigrate on their own, they may get extra points for adaptability for having a relative in Canada.

## 2.1 Sponsorship responsibilities

If you are older than 18 years of age, you can apply to sponsor your family members to join you in Canada. Sponsorship is a major, long-term commitment that cannot be taken back after the permanent residence visa is issued to your sponsored relative. Before you start the application process, you need to be aware of the responsibilities that await you as a future sponsor.

You will have to make a written commitment, which is called a Sponsorship Agreement, signed by yourself and the sponsored person, in which you promise to financially support your relative for a certain period after he or she becomes a permanent resident and the sponsored person commits to making all the efforts needed to support himself or herself. This means that you will be required to show evidence that your income is sufficient to carry out this promise. You will have to provide financial support for a period of 20 years, starting with the date the person becomes a permanent resident.

Sponsorship is a very serious commitment, and you will have to provide proof of your income before your application is accepted. Keep in mind that you cannot cancel this agreement once the visa has been granted. Moving, having a major disagreement, or no longer being able to afford to support the sponsored person do not constitute reasons for cancelling the sponsorship.

If you wish to cancel your application, you must inform the Case Processing Centre (CPC) in Mississauga in writing before the permanent resident visa is issued. After the visa is issued, the promise you made in the Sponsorship Agreement is considered valid and you cannot take it back.

## 2.2 Possible impediments to becoming a sponsor

Certain factors can keep you from becoming a sponsor. You cannot sponsor your family members if the following applies:

- You do not earn enough income to support yourself, your Canadian family members, and your sponsored relatives.

- You have recently served or are serving a prison sentence.

- You are the subject of a removal order.

- You are an undischarged bankrupt (i.e., you have not been discharged from bankruptcy proceedings).

- You have missed payments on an immigration loan or support order (e.g., alimony).

- You have been convicted of a violent or sexual crime.

- You have received government assistance (except in cases of disability).

- You have broken the terms of a previous sponsorship agreement.

# 3. Super Visa

On November 4, 2011, Citizenship and Immigration Canada (CIC) announced the temporary suspension of the Family Class sponsorship program for parents and grandparents. At the same time they introduced the new Super Visa for parents and grandparents. The Super Visa has become a permanent program to allow parents and grandparents to come temporarily to Canada, which will be valid for up to ten years and will allow them to stay in Canada for up to two years consecutively. This is an improvement over regular visitor's visas that limit stays to up to six months before visitors must apply for an extension.

The government introduced new sponsorship criteria for parents and grandparents so as to increase enhanced processing of these types of applications to prevent backlogs from happening in the future. On May 10, 2013, the Minister of Immigration has confirmed that the Super Visa will become a permanent program.

In order to be eligible to apply for a Super Visa, applicants must demonstrate that they have done the following:

- Provide proof establishing the parent or grandparent relationship to the Canadian citizen or permanent resident.

- Undergone a medical examination and are admissible to Canada on health grounds.

- Provide proof of private Canadian medical insurance valid for a minimum of one year.

- Provide proof of financial support, either from themselves or from their Canadian family members.

As is the case for other visitor's visas, immigration officers will also assess whether the person is a genuine visitor who has plans to return to his or her home country.

You can apply for the new Super Visa at visa offices outside of Canada as well as to the Case Processing Centre (CPC) inside of Canada for persons already in Canada. According to CIC, it will be able to issue the Super Visas, on average, within eight weeks of the application.

## 4. The Application Process

For the traditional sponsorship application for permanent residence, you must complete two application packages: one for sponsorship and one for permanent residence. You will apply as a sponsor, and your relative will apply for permanent residence. The sponsorship and permanent residence applications must be sent at the same time.

You'll need the following forms (http://www.cic.gc.ca/english/information/applications/sponsor-parents.asp):

1. Document Checklist — Sponsor (IMM 5771).

2. Application to Sponsor, Sponsorship Agreement and Undertaking (IMM 1344).

3. Financial Evaluation for Parents and Grandparents Sponsorship (IMM 5768).

4. Schedule A — Background/Declaration (IMM 5669).

5. Statutory Declaration of Common-Law Union (IMM 5409).

6. Generic Application Form for Canada (IMM 0008).

7. Additional Dependants/Declaration (IMM 0008DEP).

8. Additional Family Information (IMM 5406).

9. Use of a Representative (IMM 5476).

10. Fee Payment Form (IMM 5770).

You must submit your application to Mississauga, Ontario, at the Case Processing Centre (CPC):

CPC Mississauga
PO Box 6100, Station A
Mississauga, ON
L5A 4H4

Read the instructions in the application package carefully, and check once more your eligibility, and that of the person that you wish to sponsor because the processing fees are not refundable.

---

**Note:** Proof of the medical examination is a Citizenship and Immigration Canada (CIC) form that is in the application package that you take to the Designated Medical Practitioner (DMP) to complete and give to you to include in your application package. The actual medical results are sent by the DMP directly to CIC's medical branch and then transmitted to the visa officer. You must include proof that you have completed your medical examination in your application package at the outset or your application will be returned to you as incomplete. You can also send the criminal record checks as well although these can be provided at a later date if you don't have them at the outset of the application process.

---

## 4.1 Fees

The next steps are to pay the fees and mail the application. Follow the specific instructions as set out in the application package.

If you pay online, remember to print the receipt of payment form because you will need to include that in your application.

You can also pay the fees at most banks, or, if you (the sponsor) live outside Canada, you can pay with an international money order or bank draft, in Canadian funds, made out to the "Receiver General of Canada." In the latter case, you need to write the name, complete address, and account number of the bank you are using on the back of the money order or bank draft.

The fees for the family class are the following:

- Principal applicant and his or her spouse: $550 each.

- Dependant child of the principal applicant who is 18 or younger and not married or in a common-law partnership: $150 per dependant.

If the application is approved, you will also have to pay a Right of Permanent Residence Fee ($490), which is also refundable in case you withdraw your application, or you do not use your visa before its expiration date. You can pay your Right of Permanent Residence fee at any time throughout the application process. Paying this fee at the time you submit your application may speed up the application process by several weeks.

Once your sponsorship is approved — you will be notified of this by Citizenship and Immigration Canada (CIC) — the application for permanent residence of your family members will be processed. If you apply from outside Canada, Case Processing Centre (CPC) will send the application to the visa office responsible for your country.

See Chapter 3 for additional details regarding avoiding misrepresentation, reporting any change of circumstances, and the process for becoming a permanent resident.

# 5. Appealing the Decision

If you qualify as a sponsor, but the application of your family member is rejected, you may appeal to the Immigration and Appeal Division of the Immigration and Refugee Board.

If you are not approved as a sponsor, your relative may proceed with another immigration application, or apply to stay in Canada on humanitarian and compassionate grounds.

Some situations do not give you the right to an appeal, such as the following:

- Providing false or misleading information.

- Withdrawing or abandoning the sponsorship application.

- Failing to meet the eligibility criteria for spouses, partners, or dependant children.

- Existing serious criminal offence in the applicant's background.

- Security reasons such as human rights violations or involvement in organized crime.

See Chapter 13 for more information about appealing a decision.

# 10
# Canadian Experience Class

The Canadian Experience Class (CEC) was introduced in September 2008 to provide an opportunity for people who have worked temporarily or studied as international students in Canada to apply for permanent residence. After all, it makes little sense to welcome students and workers into Canada, have them contribute to the country, get accustomed to the language and culture, and then send them packing! Their experience and education in Canada gives them an advantage in their transition into becoming immigrants, which, in turn, benefits Canada as well.

This immigration class does not function on a point-based system such as for Federal Skilled Worker applicants, but rather features a pass or fail standard, meaning that applicants have to meet *all* the requirements in order to be accepted.

Those who have applied under the Federal Skilled Worker program and wish to also apply under the CEC can do so, but they will have to pay separate fees and choose under which class their residence will be granted. If their skilled worker application has not been processed at the time they apply under the CEC, they may be entitled to a refund.

> **Note:** As of January 1, 2015, the CEC will become a part of the new Express Entry program (see Chapter 12).

# 1. Temporary Foreign Workers

In order to apply for permanent residence as a temporary foreign worker, you need to have at least one year of full-time skilled work experience (or equivalent) in Canada, in an occupation at Skill Level 0 (managerial), A (professional) or B (technical), under the National Occupational Classification (NOC) (http://www.statcan.gc.ca/pub/12-583-x/12-583-x2011001-eng.pdf). Full-time work experience does not necessarily mean having one full-time job. You can accumulate part-time work experience as long as your experience is at the NOC level O, A, or B skill level and it adds up to a minimum of 30 hours of paid work experience per week.

Your authorized work experience must be acquired in the three years before you apply for residence. The keyword "authorized" is very important as any work experience gathered as an undocumented worker (i.e., without a valid work permit) is not taken into account.

If you wish to apply under this class, you must also plan to live outside the province of Quebec. Quebec has its own immigration program for selecting its immigrants so if you wish to live there, you have to conform to the requirements of its immigration system. The good news is that work experience gathered in Quebec is considered valid for the Canadian Experience Class (CEC).

If you meet the work experience requirements, but have left Canada, you can still apply for residence under the CEC from outside the country, as long as less than one year has passed since you left your Canadian job.

## 1.1 Language proficiency

The Canadian Experience Class (CEC) category has minimal language requirements depending on the National Occupational Classification (NOC) level of your occupational experience on which your language application is based. You must provide an approved language test as proof of your language ability. The language test results must not be older than two years before the time you submit your application.

The language requirements vary depending on the skill level of your occupation. For Skill Level 0 (managerial) and A (professional), you must have a minimum of seven points on the Canadian Language Benchmark (CLB) standards; for Skill Level B (technical), you only need a minimum of five points. Note that the Canadian Language Benchmark is not a test. It is a language-proficiency descriptor that visa officers use based on the evidence you provide (e.g., points scored on language tests).

The only accepted ways to prove your language ability is to take one of the following:

- English: International English Language Testing System for English (IELTS) test or

- Canadian English Language Proficiency Index Program (CELPIP).

- French: Test d'évaluation de français (TEF).

If you speak both English and French, you must choose one of them as your first language, which is the language in which you will be tested. Be sure you take the correct test for the application process you are applying for. The test for a permanent resident application may be different than for work or attending college or university. Note that you have to take the language tests even if English or French is your native tongue.

It is your responsibility to make arrangements for taking the test and to pay the necessary fees. Register and take the tests early because you cannot submit your application without the results.

If you have a spouse or common-law partner in the same situation as you (i.e., he or she meets the requirements to apply under the Canadian Experience Class), you can decide who will be the principal applicant and apply together. As adaptability points are now being awarded under the skilled worker category for a spouse's language proficiency, it is a good idea for both spouses to take the language test.

As of November 9, 2013, the CEC will not be open for certain occupations. There are also caps on the number of applications accepted in each occupation. Be sure to check the website of Citizenship and Immigration Canada (CIC) before you apply as the occupational restrictions may change from time to time.

# 2. International Student Graduates

In order to apply for permanent residence as an international student graduate, you need to have completed a study program of at least two academic years (eight months of study per year), in a Canadian postsecondary educational institution. The institution can be public or private, as long as it is accredited. Many private institutions are not accredited so check the status of your learning institution at the outset of your studies, and ensure that it is approved by Citizenship and Immigration Canada (CIC) for immigration purposes (www.cic.gc.ca/english/study/schools.asp).

At the end of your studies, you must have earned a degree, a diploma, a trade, or an apprenticeship credential from a provincially recognized public or private institution, such as a college or university or Collège d'enseignement général et professionnel (CEGEP).

Apart from the completion of the study program, you need to have at least one year of skilled, professional, or technical work experience at Skill Level O (managerial), A (professional), or B (technical), according to the National Occupational Classification (NOC) — and that year of experience must be acquired within two years of applying for residence. Just as with temporary foreign workers, you cannot let more than one year pass between your last job in Canada and the time of your application. Also, keep in mind that experience gathered without the proper authorization (i.e., no undocumented work) is not considered valid (i.e., no work permit).

Your language abilities should match the skill level of your work experience, and you need to prove this by taking one of the following tests and send your results with your application:

- English: International English Language Testing System for English (IELTS) test or

- Canadian English Language Proficiency Index Program (CELPIP).

- French: Test d'évaluation de français (TEF).

The bad news is that work experience, apprenticeships, and co-op terms completed during your study program do not count as work experience in support of a Canadian Experience Class (CEC) permanent residence application including work experience from the off-campus work permit. Only postgraduate work experience counts in the CEC application. However, graduates of Canadian medical schools will have their residency in Canada counted as work experience.

The good news for students is that as of June 1, 2014, you do not need an off-campus work permit in order to work in Canada. Students attending a designated learning institution (see Chapter 2) are eligible to work up to 20 hours per week (and full time during school breaks) without the need to obtain a work permit.

As of November 9, 2013, the CEC will not be open for certain occupations. There are also caps on the number of applications accepted in each occupation. Be sure to check CIC"s website before you apply as the occupational restrictions may change from time to time.

## 3. The Application Process

As with all the other immigration categories, the first step is to obtain an application package from the website of Citizenship and Immigration Canada (CIC) and complete the forms. The documents required include (www.cic.gc.ca/english/information/applications/cec.asp):

1. Generic Application Form for Canada (IMM 0008).

2. Additional Dependants/Declaration (IMM 0008DEP).

3. Schedule A — Background/Declaration (IMM 5669).

4. Schedule 8: Economic Classes — Canadian Experience Class (IMM 0008 SCHEDULE 8).

5. Additional Family Information (IMM 5406).

6. Separation Declaration for Minors Travelling to Canada (IMM 5604).

7. Statutory Declaration of Common-law Union (IMM 5409).

8. Fee Payment Form — Application for Permanent Residence (IMM 5620).

9. Use of a Representative (IMM 5476).

10. Document Checklist (IMM 5610).

Remember to include your language test results in the envelope with your application. This is the only chance you get to prove your language abilities since there will be no interview.

If the application is not complete, it will be returned to you. As mentioned in Chapter 3, do not fill in any misleading or inaccurate information as that may result in your becoming inadmissible to Canada.

## 3.1 Fees

The next steps are to pay the fees and mail your application along with your language test results. If you pay online, remember to print the receipt of payment form because you will need to include that in your application.

You can pay the fees at most banks, or, if you live outside Canada, you can pay with an international money order or bank draft, in Canadian funds, made out to the "Receiver General for Canada." In the latter case, you need to write the name, complete address, and account number of the bank you are using on the back of the money order or bank draft.

You will have to pay a processing fee for you and your spouse ($550 each) as well as your dependants aged 18 or younger ($150 each). These fees are refundable if your application is found to be ineligible. Be sure to include the correct application fees for you and your dependants. If you fail to include the correct fee payment, your application will be considered incomplete and returned to you.

You must submit your application to the following address:

Citizenship and Immigration Canada
Canadian Experience Class
Centralized Intake Office
PO Box 4000
Sydney, NS
B1P 1J3
Canada

Applicants from outside Canada must send their application to the visa office responsible for their home country, and find out what are the accepted methods of payment. This information can usually be found on the websites of the respective visa offices (www.cic.gc.ca/english/information/offices/missions.asp).

# 11
# Federal Skilled Trades Class

For many years now, Canada has been facing a significant shortage of skilled tradespeople. More and more Canadian youth are pursuing higher education, but the focus has been toward college and university rather than encouraging them to pursue careers in the trades. Also with Canada's aging population, many of the experienced tradespeople are now retiring and a considerable shortage of tradespeople has developed.

In order to address Canada's current and impending shortage in the skilled trades, on January 2, 2013, Canada's Minister of Immigration introduced the new Federal Skilled Trades Class (FSTC) (http://www.cic.gc.ca/english/immigrate/trades/).

> **Note:** As of January 1, 2015, the FSTC will become a part of the new Express Entry program (see Chapter 12).

## 1. Federal Skilled Trades Criteria

In order to be eligible to apply under the Federal Skilled Trades Class (FSTC), you must do the following:

- Intend to reside in a province or territory other than Quebec.

- Meet the prescribed language proficiency in either English or French in each of the language skill areas (i.e., reading, writing, speaking, and listening).

- Have acquired at least two years of full-time work experience, or the equivalent of part-time work experience, in a skilled trade within the past five years preceding the date of your application.

- Meet the employment requirements of an eligible trade as set out in the National Occupational Classification (NOC); except for meeting the requirement of the provincial or territorial licensing requirements for that trade. Have arranged employment with a specific employer or possess a provincial or territorial certificate of qualification in a skilled trade.

Not all trades are eligible for an application under this new FSTC category. As was discussed in previous chapters, Canada has developed a considerable backlog of applications for permanent residence over the years, which has caused applicants to face serious delays in the processing of their applications. In order to avoid future backlogs and to facilitate speedy processing times, the FSTC accepted only 3,000 applications in its first year of operation from January 2, 2013, to January 1, 2014, with eligible applicants being categorized into two categories — Group A and Group B applicants. However, as of May 1, 2014 this distinction has been eliminated.

The Minister of Immigration has announced an increase in the total applications accepted under the FSTC as well as the number of trades that are eligible to apply under the program. Starting from May 1, 2014, until April 30, 2015, the program will accept a total of 5,000 skilled trades applications. There is also a cap of 100 applications for each trade eligible to apply under the program. For a complete list of eligible trades please see the Government of Canada's website (http://www.cic.gc.ca/english/immigrate/trades/applications.asp).

## 1.1 Language proficiency

You have to meet the minimal language requirements for your skill level and you must provide an approved language test as proof of your language ability. The language test results must not be older than two years before the time you submit your application.

Citizenship and Immigration Canada (CIC) assesses proficiency in accordance with the Canadian Language Benchmark (CLB) standards. Note that the CLB is not a test. It is a language-proficiency descriptor that visa officers use based on the evidence you provide (e.g., points scored on language tests).

The language proficiency level for the Federal Skilled Trades Class (FSTC) category is currently set at CLB 5 for speaking and listening and CLB 4 for reading and writing. You must include the results of a recognized language-testing service, which demonstrates your language proficiency in all four language skill areas of reading, writing, speaking and listening. You can check the current language proficiency requirement here (www.cic.gc.ca/english/immigrate/trades/language.asp).

The CLB levels are set for each testing service so if you want to make sure your language test scores are good enough to meet the program requirements, you can check this in the immigration manuals (http://www.cic.gc.ca/english/resources/manuals/op/op26-eng.pdf).

Acceptance in the FSTC is based on a pass-fail system. In order to be considered a member of this class, you must do the following:

- Satisfy the language proficiency requirements: CLB 5 for speaking and listening and CLB 4 for reading and writing.

- Show that you have acquired at least two years of full-time work experience (or equivalent part-time work experience) within the past five years just before submitting your application and your work experience must have been acquired after becoming qualified to practice your trade.

- Meet the specified employer requirements of your skilled trade as set out in the National Occupational Classification (NOC) description (except for the need to meet provincial or territorial licensing requirements).

- Have an offer of employment from a Canadian employer for at least one year of full-time work in your skilled trade or have a certificate of qualification in a skilled trade from a Canadian provincial or territorial apprenticeship body.

If you do not meet these specific requirements, your application will be refused. You want to be very careful in evaluating your language ability and work experience in order to ensure you meet and will pass the test for acceptance in the FSTC. Many trades in Canada require a licence before you are able to work. CIC permits applicants under the FSTC to obtain their permanent residence status without obtaining the necessary licence prior to immigrating to Canada. However, you will need to factor the time it will take to obtain your licence as a consideration for your initial stay when you arrive as you may not be able to support yourself and your family until you obtain your licence. You should check to see whether licensing is required for your particular trade for the province or territory in which you intend to reside. Contact the licensing body to determine what steps you will need to take and try and complete as many as possible before you arrive to be able to obtain your licence sooner.

## 2. The Application Process

As with all the other immigration categories, the first step is to obtain an application package from the Citizenship and Immigration Canada (CIC) website and complete the forms. Attach the required documentation and mail in your application. The documents required include the following (http://www.cic.gc.ca/english/information/applications/guides/5747ETOC.asp):

1. Document Checklist — Federal Skilled Trades Class (IMM 5750).

2. Generic Application Form for Canada (IMM 0008).

3. Additional Dependants/Declaration (IMM 0008DEP).

4. Schedule A: Background/Declaration (IMM 5669).

5. Schedule 11: Economic Classes — Federal Skilled Trades Class (IMM 0008 SCHEDULE 11).

6. Additional Family Information (IMM 5406).

7. Supplementary Information — Your travels (IMM 5562.

8. Separation Declaration for Minors Travelling to Canada (MM 5604).

9. Statutory Declaration of Common-Law Union (IMM 5409).

10. Fee Payment Form — Application for Permanent Residence (IMM 5620).

11. Use of a Representative (IMM 5476).

Remember to include your language test results in the envelope with your application. This is the only chance you get to prove your language abilities since there will be no interview.

If the application is not complete, it will be returned to you. As mentioned in Chapter 3, do not fill in any misleading or inaccurate information as that may result in your becoming inadmissible to Canada.

## 2.1 Fees

The next steps are to pay the fees and mail your application along with your language test results. Please see payment instructions on the Citizenship and Immigration Canada (CIC) website. If you pay online, remember to print the receipt of payment form because you will need to include that in your application.

You can also pay the fees at most banks, or, if you (the sponsor) live outside Canada, you can pay with an international money order or bank draft, in Canadian funds, made out to the "Receiver General for Canada." In the latter case, you need to write the name, complete address, and account number of the bank you are using on the back of the money order or bank draft.

You will have to pay a processing fee for you and your spouse ($550 each) and your adult dependants ($550 each) as well as your dependants aged 18 or younger ($150). These fees are refundable if your application is found to be ineligible. Be sure to include the correct application fees for you and your dependants. If you fail to include the correct fee payment, your application will be considered incomplete and returned to you.

You must submit your application to the following address:

Citizenship and Immigration Canada
Federal Skilled trades
Centralized Intake Office
PO Box 8600
Sydney, NS
B1P 0G1

See Chapter 3 for additional details regarding avoiding misrepresentation, reporting any change of circumstances, and the process for becoming a permanent resident.

# 12
## Express Entry: Canada's Future Immigration Program

The government will launch an active recruitment model known as the Express Entry system in early 2015. This system is intended to help switch from the passive processing of applications in the order that Citizenship and Immigration Canada (CIC) receive them to one that prioritizes processing for people with the skills to succeed in Canada.

Historically Canada's economic immigration program was an applicant-driven responsive program. People who decided that they wanted to immigrate to Canada submitted an application and the government was bound to consider and assess that application. The number of applications received was always far greater than the number of applications that the government could process and over time a considerable backlog developed for the skilled worker, entrepreneur, and investor applicants which ultimately led to the suspension of these categories. The skilled worker program was eventually re-opened in 2013 with significant changes to it but the investor and entrepreneur categories have been formally terminated.

Express Entry will no longer be an applicant-driven responsive program. Rather it will transform Canada's immigration system to one that is fast, flexible, and focused on meeting Canada's economic and labour needs. Formerly referred to as "Expression of Interest" this new process will allow skilled immigrants to electronically provide preliminary information to the government regarding their education, skills, work experience, and language proficiency as well as other biographical data. The information that applicants provide will be assessed on a "human capital grid," which has not yet been established or published. Based on applicants' human capital score, they will be invited to submit an electronic application for permanent residence. Only the best applicants or those that match with a specific employer's requirements will be invited to submit an application.

Express Entry will apply to the following economic categories of immigration:

- Federal Skilled Worker Program (FSWP).

- Federal Skilled Trades Program (FSTP).

- Canadian Experience Class (CEC).

- Provincial Nominee Programs (PCP).

Express Entry will be a mandatory first step in these categories.

Provinces and territories will have the option to use Express Entry to identify additional provincial and territorial nominees for the Provincial Nominee Programs (PNPs) over and above their provincial or territorial nomination allocations to an overall and by-jurisdiction limit. Under the Express Entry system, qualified applicants can expect faster processing times of six months or less when they are invited to submit an application. In addition, employers will have a key role in selecting economic immigrants and in providing input and advice about the program to the Canadian government.

Here are some quick facts about the Express Entry program:

- The Government of Canada's new and improved Job Bank will help facilitate matches between Canadian employers and Express Entry candidates.

- Canada will be able to select the best candidates who are most likely to achieve success in Canada, rather than the first person in line.

- Having a valid job offer or a provincial or territorial nomination will guarantee candidates an invitation to apply for Express Entry.

- Canada's Economic Action Plan 2014 will invest $14 million over two years and $4.7 million per year ongoing to ensure the successful implementation of Express Entry.

The Express Entry system will significantly change Canada's immigration program. Economic immigration has had restrictions placed on it in recent years (e.g., what occupations are eligible and caps on the number of applications to be accepted); if a person met the qualifications for the program, his or her application would be processed and he or she would be granted permanent resident status. What is dramatically different is that not all eligible applicants will be invited to apply for permanent residence — only the very best applicants! There is now a qualitative component to Canada's immigration program. The positive tradeoff is that applications will be processed in six months or less rather than over several years.

Express Entry will help Canada's economy and it will revolutionize the way Canada attracts skilled immigrants and gets them working here faster. Our government is actively engaging with our provincial and territorial partners, and with employers, to make the launch of Express Entry a success.

Be sure to stay tuned to the CIC's website to learn more about the new Express Entry program as it develops and the details unfold.

# 13
# Challenging a Refusal

No one likes to think of the worst-case scenario, but the fact is some applications get rejected and this is an extremely frustrating situation if you have your heart set on Canada. If you get a negative answer, you should know that you have the possibility to file an appeal or application for judicial review.

An *appeal* challenges Citizenship and Immigration Canada"s (CIC) refusal of your application in front of the Immigration Appeal Division (IAD) of the Immigration and Refugee Board (IRB). A *judicial review* application can be filed to challenge the decision of the IRB after obtaining permission from the Federal Court of Canada. Only certain types of refusals may pursue an appeal at the IAD; all others can pursue judicial review by the Federal Court of Canada.

> **Note:** It is strongly recommended that you consult an immigration lawyer before you start the process to see if your appeal or judicial review application has a good chance of success.

## 1. Appeals

You can represent yourself, or be represented by counsel, consultant, relative, friend, or trusted member of your community. If your counsel charges a fee for representing you, he or she must be a member in good standing of the Immigration Consultants of Canada Regulatory Council (ICCRC), a provincial or territorial law society; or the Chambre des notaires du Québec.

Appeal hearings are public and are handled by the Immigration and Refugee Board (IRB). The final decision will be made by a member of the Immigration Appeal Division (IAD) of the IRB. The person arguing against your appeal will be a Minister's Counsel from the Canada Border Services Agency (CBSA).

The IAD deals with the following types of appeals:

- Sponsorship appeals.

- Appeals from a removal order issued by an officer of the CBSA or the IRB.

- Residency obligation appeals.

- Minister's appeal of an Immigration Division decision.

It usually takes the IAD between eight to ten months to schedule a hearing for an immigration appeal. The decision may be made at the hearing or at a later date.

## 1.1 Sponsorship cases

Sponsorship applicants whose application has been rejected by Citizenship and Immigration Canada (CIC) appeal the decision. However, you cannot appeal if you withdrew or abandoned your sponsorship application, or if the family members you wish to sponsor have been found inadmissible to Canada based on misrepresentation or security grounds.

If the appeal is allowed, CIC will either resume processing the sponsorship application, or it may apply for a judicial review of the Immigration Appeal Division (IAD) decision after obtaining permission from the Federal Court of Canada.

Keep in mind that having an appeal allowed does not mean that the permanent residence visa is guaranteed. CIC could still reject the application on other grounds. If the appeal is dismissed, the sponsor can ask permission from the Federal Court of Canada to contest the IAD decision.

## 1.2 Appeals of removal orders

Only permanent residents are able to make an appeal of a removal order to the Immigration Appeal Division (IAD). Persons subject to a removal order (e.g., exclusion or deportation order) can apply to the Federal Court for judicial review, unless they have been found inadmissible to Canada based on security grounds, they are foreign nationals without a permanent resident visa, or they are refugee claimants whose claim has been rejected.

If the appeal is allowed, you will get permission to stay in Canada. However, you will have to provide updated application forms which could take a further 6 to 12 months.

If the appeal is dismissed, the Canada Border Services Agency (CBSA) may remove you from Canada. The IAD decision can be contested after obtaining permission from the Federal Court of Canada to apply for judicial review.

If the IAD stays the appeal (i.e., it suspends the effect of the removal order for a period of time), you may be allowed to remain in Canada under certain conditions decided by the IAD. The stay of the removal order can be cancelled at any time, or the IAD may change its conditions or duration. Breaking the conditions of the stay will automatically cancel it and it may even lead to deportation without the chance of a hearing. If the conditions of the stay are fulfilled for its entire duration, the removal order will be cancelled at the end of the time period.

If you are representing yourself, you should consult the IAD rules to make sure that you conform to the specific requirements of the tribunal: http://www.irb-cisr.gc.ca/Eng/ImmApp/pages/IadSai.aspx

## 1.3 Residency appeals

After you receive permanent resident status in Canada, you have certain obligations to meet, including living in Canada for at least two years within a five-year period. Permanent residents who have not fulfilled their residency obligation and are stripped of their permanent residency status can appeal to the Immigration Appeal Division (IAD). If the IAD decides that you must be physically present at the hearing, a Citizenship and Immigration Canada (CIC) officer will issue a travel document allowing you to return to Canada for this occasion.

If the appeal is allowed, you will keep your permanent resident status. If the appeal is dismissed, you will lose your permanent resident status, but you can still contest the IAD decision, after obtaining permission from the Federal Court of Canada to apply for judicial review.

## 1.4 Why appeals are allowed

Appeals are allowed if the refusal decision made by Citizenship and Immigration Canada (CIC) or the Canada Border Services Agency (CBSA) was wrong in law or fact, if there was a breach of a principle of natural justice, or on humanitarian and compassionate grounds. You have the responsibility to show why your appeal should be allowed, and provide all the necessary evidence to support your arguments.

## 1.5 Disclosure of documents

Any documentary evidence used in the appeal has to be made available to all parties involved in the appeal hearing, within the appropriate time frames. This process is called "disclosure" and it is essential that you disclose your documents properly; otherwise, you may not be able to use them at the hearing.

If you are representing yourself, you should consult the Immigration Appeal Division (IAD) rules to make sure that you conform to the specific requirements of this tribunal (http://www.irb-cisr.gc.ca/Eng/ImmApp/pages/IadSai.aspx).

You must make two copies of each document you plan to use in the appeal hearing, and send one to the Minister's Counsel at Canada Border Services Agency (CBSA) and one to the IAD registry office. The copies have to be received no later than 20 days before the scheduled date for the appeal hearing. Within the same time frame, the Minister's Counsel will send you the appeal record, which contains the Citizenship and Immigration Canada (CIC) or CBSA documents related to your case. After receiving the documents from the Minister's Counsel, you can provide other documents in response to them, but no later than ten days before the hearing.

Needless to say, you should have all the necessary documents and information ready as soon as possible to avoid any unpleasant surprises. Use a reliable courier service to deliver your documents, especially if you are behind schedule.

## 1.6 Alternative Dispute Resolution

Alternative Dispute Resolution (ADR) is a more informal approach, which offers the chance of settling the appeal in a consensual, less confrontational way. Most often, ADR is used in certain cases of sponsorship appeals and it is discretionary, meaning that the Immigration Appeal Division (IAD) may select an appeal for ADR based on the strength of the case.

The appellant, his or her counsel, and the Minister's Counsel will have an in-person meeting, which lasts for approximately an hour. This meeting is called an ADR conference and it will be conducted by a Dispute Resolution Officer (DRO) who will assist the appellant and the Minister's Counsel to reach an agreement. If you feel that your case is very strong, you may request an ADR hearing in order to resolve the matter without the need for a full hearing. If the case is resolved at the ADR hearing, your case will continue to be processed by Citizenship and Immigration Canada (CIC). If you are not successful at ADR, you have the ability to proceed to a full hearing.

## 1.7 Changing the date of an appeal hearing

If you or your counsel cannot be present at the appeal hearing on the scheduled date, you need to make a written application (i.e., a letter) requesting for a postponement or adjournment. As with all the documents involved in an appeal, you need to send a copy to the Immigration Appeal Division (IAD) and one to the Minister's Counsel.

In the postponement application, you have to give the reasons you cannot be present on the initially scheduled date, say whether the Minister's Counsel agrees with your request, and suggest at least six new dates in which you can be present at the hearing. You should contact the IAD registry office to see which weeks or months the IAD has available for hearings, and set the six alternate dates within that period.

The IAD will take into account only very serious reasons for changing the date of an appeal hearing. If your application is rejected, or if you do not get any answer from the IAD, you must show up at the initially scheduled date and be prepared for the appeal. Your appeal may be dismissed if you fail to show up.

Do not wait too long if you wish to postpone the date of your hearing. If the IAD or the Minister's Counsel receives your postponement application two working days or less before the scheduled date, it is too late. You will have to appear on the scheduled date and be prepared to argue your case. You may still ask for a postponement at that time, but you have no guarantee that your request will be granted.

## 1.8 Bringing witnesses

If you wish to bring witnesses to testify for you at the appeal hearing, you must provide information about them to the Immigration Appeal Division (IAD) and the Minister's Counsel no later than 20 days before the scheduled date for the hearing. The information should be provided in writing and include the following:

- Witness's contact information.

- Your relationship to the witness.

- How long the testimony will take.

- Whether it will be in person, by telephone, or by video conference.

In the case of expert witnesses, you must also have them sign a report listing their qualifications and summarizing their evidence. You will need to send this report to the IAD and the Minister's Counsel. Failing to provide all the required information before the time limit may result in the IAD deciding not to accept your witness's testimony.

You may ask the IAD registry office for a summons, in case you are worried that your witness may not show up at the hearing. A summons is an IAD order to appear at the hearing that the witness must obey. You can get all the necessary information about summons rules from the IAD registry office.

If your witness is not in Canada, he or she may testify by telephone if the IAD allows it. You must inform the IAD about this before the hearing, and it is your responsibility to pay for the call and to make sure that the witness can be reached at the time of the hearing. You will need to bring with you a calling card from your telephone company or a long-distance phone card, with at least two hours of international calling time available. Make sure you pick a reliable type of card; sometimes there are problems with the long-distance calls, and the IAD may decide to do without your witness and move on with the hearing.

## 1.9 Translations and interpreting

The documents you plan to use for your appeal hearing need to be translated by a certified translator if they are not in English or French. You will have to provide the copies of the documents, the translations, and a translator's declaration to the Immigration Appeal Division (IAD) and the Minister's Counsel. The translator's declaration will include the translator's name, the language translated, and a signed statement that the translation is accurate. At the appeal hearing, you should also bring the original documents with you.

If you or your witnesses need an interpreter, you should notify the IAD registry office at the scheduling conference, or in writing, no later than 20 days before the scheduled appeal hearing, and indicate the language or dialect that is needed. The interpreter will be provided by the IAD at no charge to you.

## 1.10 Steps of an appeal

You will be notified by the Immigration Appeal Division (IAD) to take part in a scheduling conference (Assignment Court), together with your counsel, if you have one. An IAD member will ask questions to see if your case is ready for scheduling. If it is, you will be given the date and time of the appeal hearing.

At the appeal hearing, you will have to answer the questions asked by your counsel, if you have one, and by the Minister's Counsel who is there to argue against your case. If you do not have counsel, you may say what you think is relevant to your case, or ask the IAD member to ask you questions that he or she believes are relevant.

The witnesses will stay in a waiting room and will be asked to join the hearing only after your testimony. At the beginning of the hearing, the IAD member will ask them to solemnly promise that they will tell the truth. Subsequently, you, your counsel, the Minister's Counsel, or the IAD member can question the witnesses present.

Once all the testimony has been given, you or your counsel will be asked to make your argument and explain why the evidence presented should determine the IAD member to allow your appeal. Then, the Minister's Counsel will be asked to make his or her argument, and you or your counsel will be asked to respond to it.

In some cases, you may receive the decision of the IAD member at the end of the hearing, together with an explanation of the reasons. Otherwise, you will receive the decision by mail, usually no later than 90 days from the date of the appeal hearing.

Given the significance and complexity of an appeal, it is strongly advisable that you use the services of an immigration lawyer.

## 2. Applying for a Judicial Review

In order to contest an Immigration and Refugee Board (IRB) decision, you need to file an Application for Leave and Judicial Review with the Federal Court of Canada, no later than 15 days after being notified of the IRB decision. To obtain the leave permission of the court, you will have to show the court that there is a serious issue to be determined such as an error of law or fact has been made, or that a principle of natural justice has been breached.

Judicial review is not like an appeal. The judge at the Federal Court cannot substitute his or her opinion for that of the decision maker, but can only review the decision to see whether it was made in accordance with the law or the principles of natural justice. If not, the judge will set aside the decision and have the matter sent back to be considered by another decision maker.

The Federal Court process is a judicial proceeding and it is highly recommended that you have legal representation. If you decide that you want representation, only a lawyer can represent you in Federal Court, not an authorized immigration consultant.

# 14
# You're Approved! Now What?

Immigrating to Canada is probably one of the biggest decisions you have ever had to make. After dealing with the paperwork, the fees, and the long months of waiting, the much-anticipated visa is finally in your hands! Congratulations!

Of course, you should celebrate this milestone, but don't forget your journey has really only just begun. The true journey begins after you land in Canada, and it can be a challenging, confusing process. That's why I wrote the book *Arrival Survival Canada* (http://www.arrivalsurvival.com/). After experiencing this journey myself, I wanted to help other newcomers settle in faster. The book has become a bestseller, but its focus is on post-arrival. I later realized that immigrants also need to know more information before they get on the plane, from applying to waiting to preparing, which is why I wanted to write this prequel, if you will. So, the next few chapters are all about what you need to understand after your visa has been approved, but before you finally arrive on Canadian soil.

First things first, there are many things to decide, plan, and learn, starting with choosing a province or territory and city in which to settle, what to bring with you, and arranging temporary accommodation for your first few nights.

# 1. Choose a Location

Some immigrants prefer cities where they already have friends or relatives who can guide their first steps in Canada. Others do not have anyone waiting for them so they have to decide which province or territory and city or town to choose based only on research. One thing is certain, most immigrants have traditionally favoured the big cities such as Vancouver, Toronto, and Montreal.

When choosing the right location for you, you have to take into account factors such as climate, languages spoken, taxes, health services, cost of living, schools, and ethnic and religious diversity. It is not always an easy decision to make, but remember that you always have the possibility to relocate if you are not satisfied with your choice. (See Chapter 15.)

Medium and large cities generally offer more job opportunities, more cultural diversity, and more excitement. Small cities have a lower cost of living and are less stressful. The gorgeous landscapes of rural Canada may also be appealing to you. Up to 30 percent of Canada's population lives in rural areas or small towns.

After you choose a place, it is a good idea to find and contact an immigrant services organization. These organizations are supported by Citizenship and Immigration Canada (CIC), and their purpose is to help newcomers adapt to life in Canada. You can find a list of immigrant service organizations on the Government of Canada's website (http://www.cic.gc.ca/english/newcomers/map/services.asp).

## 1.1 Industries by location

The right location for you may very well depend on whether it's a good fit for your career. While certain jobs and industries can be found across the country (i.e., health care and tourism), some areas are better suited for certain fields than others. For example, if you want to find work in the automotive industry or manufacturing, you would focus on Ontario. Big finance is concentrated in Toronto. Agriculture-related jobs are more common in Manitoba, Saskatchewan, and Alberta. The oil and gas industry is focused in Alberta primarily, while the forestry industry is largely in British Columbia.

## 1.2  French-speaking regions

If you wish to live in a francophone community, you should know that there are choices outside of Quebec. The largest francophone populations outside Quebec are in Ontario (more than 578,000), New Brunswick (more than 236,000), British Columbia (more than 70,000), Alberta (more than 66,000), Manitoba (more than 44,000), and Nova Scotia (more than 32,000). If French is your first language, you should consider the option for immigration to Quebec.

# 2.  Present Your Documents to Citizenship and Immigration (CIC)

When you arrive in Canada, you will have to present some documents to the Citizenship and Immigration (CIC) officers. You will need to have the following documents with you:

- Valid passport and travel documents for each family member.

- Immigrant visa and the Confirmation of Permanent Residence (COPR) document for each family member.

- Two copies of a detailed list of all the items you and your family are bringing with you and the value of the items.

- Two copies of a detailed list of items you plan to have sent later, or that are already on their way, and their value.

You can list your personal belongings on a special Personal Effects Accounting Document (B4 form) that can be downloaded from the Canada Border Services Agency (CBSA) website (www.cbsa.gc.ca).

The following are other documents you and your family members should bring:

- Diplomas, certificates, school records, employer reference letters, trade licenses — you may need them in order to get your credentials evaluated, get a job, or attend school.

- Adoption papers.

- Marriage, divorce, or separation papers.

- Driver's licence, International Driver's Permit, references from your auto insurance company.

- Vehicle registration documents, if you're importing a vehicle.

- Financial records and proof of credit history.

- Birth certificates and baptismal certificates.

Make photocopies of all these documents, in case the originals get lost or destroyed. Consider having all your important papers translated into English or French. You may need them later, and translation services are quite costly in Canada.

Remember to pack these essential documents in your hand luggage because you will need them before you can retrieve your suitcase.

## 2.1 Proof of funds

You may also be asked to provide evidence that you have the minimum funds necessary to support yourself and your family for six months. If you are bringing more than $10,000 Canadian, which can be in the form of cash, stocks, bonds, treasury bills, debentures, money orders, bankers' drafts, travellers' cheques, money orders, or cheques, you have to disclose that to the immigration officer, otherwise you may be fined or imprisoned.

## 2.2 Health-care documents

It is very important to bring your and your family's health-care documents to prove that you have been vaccinated (immunized). Your children will not be able to enroll in school if they have not been properly vaccinated.

# 3. Customs and Declarations

You may be asked to fill in a Customs Declaration Card before you meet with the immigration officers. You should fill in this declaration before you leave the airplane. Mention any items that you must pay duty on, including alcohol, tobacco and gifts; and any business goods, plants, food, animals, firearms or other weapons, and any amount of money more than $10,000 Canadian that you are bringing into Canada.

## 3.1 Permitted and forbidden goods

Canadian laws are very strict when it comes to what you can bring into the country. You have to make sure you do not bring any forbidden items because they will be taken away from you by the customs personnel, and you may end up in an unpleasant situation. The Canada Border Services Agency (CBSA) website has detailed explanations about what you can and cannot bring into Canada. Forbidden goods include the following:

- Firearms, explosives, fireworks, and ammunition.

- Narcotics other than prescription drugs.

- Meat, dairy products, and fresh fruits and vegetables.

- Plants, flowers, and soil.

- Endangered species of animals or products made from animal parts (i.e., skin, feathers, fur, bones, and ivory).

- Cultural property, including antique and cultural objects considered to have historical significance in their country of origin (you may, however, bring family heirlooms).

- More than 200 cigarettes (you must pay tax on the excess amount) per person 18 years of age or older if you are immigrating to Quebec, Alberta, Saskatchewan, or Manitoba, or per person 19 years of age or older if you are immigrating to Ontario or any of the other provinces and territories.

- More than 1.5 litres of wine or 1.14 litres of alcohol (you must pay tax on the excess amount) per person 18 years of age or older.

If you wish to bring pets into Canada, you must first check the guidelines set by the Canadian Food Inspection Agency (www. inspection.gc.ca/animals/terrestrial-animals/imports/policies/ live-animals/pet-imports/eng/1326600389775/1326600500578.

There are specific guidelines for bringing in pets and, if not met, they can be refused entry. While cats and dogs do not need to be quarantined, you do have to provide proof of their age and that all necessary vaccinations are up-to-date. You should decide this well in advance of your move to Canada.

## 3.2 Paying duty

When you come to Canada, you will have to pay duty on certain items. Your personal belongings are duty free, but if you want to purchase things from the duty-free shops you visit, you should consider that gifts of more than $60 can be taxed. Also, take into account the limits imposed on alcohol and cigarettes as mentioned earlier.

Goods you have to pay duty on include the following:

- Items you have leased or rented (the Canada Border Services Agency does not consider that you own leased or rented items).
- Items you have bought on your way to Canada.
- Vehicles you plan to use for business.
- Farm equipment.
- Equipment you plan to use in construction, contracting, or manufacturing.

Goods you do not have to pay duty on include the following:

- Antiques.
- Appliances and electronics.
- Books.
- Clothes.
- Furniture.
- Hobby tools and items.
- Jewellery.
- Linens.
- Musical instruments.
- Private collections of coins, stamps, and art.
- Silverware.
- Gifts each worth $60 Canadian or more.

## 3.3 Bringing a vehicle into Canada

If you wish to bring a vehicle into Canada, you must check to see that it meets the safety and pollution standards of Canada. Contact

Transport Canada to avoid any unpleasant surprises. See Transport Canada's website for more information (www.tc.gc.ca).

## 3.4 Interview at customs

Before you are allowed entry into Canada, you will have to go through two screening interviews with one or two immigration officers. During the first interview, the officer will check your visa and travel documents and ask you about your health, criminal history, and the funds that you are bringing with you. If everything is in order, you will go to the second interview where the officer will check the Personal Effects Accounting Document (B4 form) of items you are bringing into Canada and items that will arrive later. The officer may also ask to inspect your luggage.

Give complete and truthful answers because it is a serious offence to lie to an immigration officer. This may result in fines, imprisonment, or cancellation of your visa.

Once everything has been verified, the officer will sign your Confirmation of Permanent Residence (COPR) document and you will be allowed to enter Canada as a permanent resident. Be sure to save this document as you will need it to renew your permanent resident card or apply for Canadian citizenship.

## 4. Temporary Accommodation

For your first night in Canada, you will hopefully have arranged a place to stay before you left your country of origin. Most people stay with friends or relatives in Canada, or temporary accommodation in hotels or motels.

Some hotels and motels offer monthly rates, which will be far more affordable than paying nightly rates, which are usually $100 or more per night. Other options for temporary stays include local YMCAs and hostels.

# 15
## An Overview of Canada

How much do you really know about Canada and its people? This chapter takes a look at some basic facts about Canada.

Around the world, Canada is known for a lot of things such as abundant forests and wildlife, cold winters, Mounties in red uniforms, maple syrup, polite citizens, and universal health care (note that health care is not totally free).

Famous Canadians you may have heard of include Terry Fox, Pierre Trudeau, Pamela Anderson, David Suzuki, Celine Dion, Michael Bublé, Bryan Adams, Jim Carrey, and Shania Twain.

You may have also heard that it was a Canadian who invented basketball, a Canadian who first used insulin to treat diabetes, and a Canadian who patented the first lightbulb.

Moving to a new country is a big gamble and takes a lot of courage. Taking the time to learn what to expect — and what is expected of you — *before* you arrive can help your immigration journey become a success.

# 1. Canadian Provinces and Territories

Canada is made up of ten provinces and three territories. It can also be divided into five regional areas:

- The East, also called the Atlantic region, includes the provinces of Newfoundland and Labrador, Nova Scotia, New Brunswick, and Prince Edward Island.

- The Central region includes the provinces of Quebec and Ontario.

- The Prairies include Manitoba, Saskatchewan, and some parts of Alberta.

- The West includes most of Alberta and British Columbia.

- The North is made up of the three territories: Nunavut, Yukon, and the Northwest Territories.

The national capital of Canada is Ottawa, Ontario. Each province and territory has its own capital city where the provincial or territorial government is located, as shown in Table 13.

### Table 13
### CAPITAL CITIES

| Province/Territory | Capital City |
|---|---|
| British Columbia | Victoria |
| Alberta | Edmonton |
| Saskatchewan | Regina |
| Manitoba | Winnipeg |
| Ontario | Toronto |
| Quebec | Quebec City |
| New Brunswick | Fredericton |
| Nova Scotia | Halifax |
| Prince Edward Island | Charlottetown |
| Newfoundland and Labrador | St. John's |
| Nunavut | Iqaluit |
| Northwest Territories | Yellowknife |
| Yukon | Whitehorse |

## 2. The Canadian Landscape

Canada is an enormous country. It is very diverse in its landscape, climate, people, and way of life. It has a total land area of 9,984,670 square kilometres, making it the second largest country in the world. The longest distance north to south (on land) is 4,634 kilometers, from the northern tip of Nunavut to the southern tip of Ontario. The longest distance east to west is 5,514 kilometres from the eastern tip of Newfoundland and Labrador to the western tip of the Yukon Territory where it borders with Alaska.

To help you better appreciate the sheer size of this country, consider this: It takes seven days to drive from Halifax, Nova Scotia, to Vancouver, British Columbia. Flying from Halifax to Vancouver takes seven hours. More proof of this country's immense size: Canada has six separate time zones — Newfoundland, Atlantic, Eastern, Central, Mountain, and Pacific.

### 2.1 Canada's natural resources

Canada's forests, wildlife, protected areas, and water are well known around the world. In the days of the first settlers, Canada grew quickly as a result of such natural resources. From the trade of beaver pelts to the longstanding logging industry, the country was built on the bounty of the land. Images of lumberjacks and beaver pelt hats are truly iconic Canadian images.

Today, Canada has more than 71,500 known species of plants and wild animals. It contains 20 percent of the world's remaining wilderness and 10 percent of the world's forests. Canada has 7 percent of the world's renewable freshwater supply and 25 percent of the world's wetlands.

Surrounded by nature and wildlife, Canadians are especially conscious of the need to respect and protect the environment for the future. There are some simple things we all can do to work toward a sustainable future, such as participating in recycling programs; reducing energy consumption; keeping parks and streets clean by putting garbage into garbage cans; and using public transportation, riding a bicycle, or walking rather than using a vehicle.

### 2.2 Climate from coast to coast

Because of the distance from one coast to the other, the climate or weather differs greatly across the country. Many factors influence weather, such as distance from the ocean, latitude, elevation, and wind. You may want to consider these differences when choosing a place to live.

Northern and central regions can be very cold and snowy in the winter with temperatures dropping lower than zero degrees Celsius. With the wind-chill factor, temperatures have been recorded as low as minus 40 degrees Celsius in cities such as Toronto, Ontario; Regina, Saskatchewan; Winnipeg, Manitoba, and Edmonton, Alberta. Those same areas can see highs of 40 degrees Celsius in the summer months.

On the coasts, weather is generally milder. In Vancouver, British Columbia, for example, winters feature more rain than snow. However, rain also makes a frequent appearance in the warmer summer months, too.

Despite the variances in temperatures across the country, all regions have four distinct seasons in Canada: winter, spring, summer, and autumn (also called "fall").

### 2.2a  Spring: March 21 to June 21

This is the season when the winter snow begins to melt. Often, there is a lot of rain during this period as the days become warmer and longer, and the nights remain cool. Plants begin to grow in spring. In most parts of Canada, trees remain bare until April or May.

- **What to wear:** You will need a warm coat. An umbrella is also recommended.

- **What to do:** Go out and enjoy nature in spring. There are plenty of activities to take part in, from golf to hiking. It's also a good time for spring cleaning at home.

### 2.2b  Summer: June 21 to September 21

Temperatures can reach 40 degrees Celsius or higher during summer as the weather becomes hot and dry. Some areas, especially near the Great Lakes in Ontario, experience humid air and thunderstorms. Most regions experience mosquitoes in late spring or early summer. In many areas, especially rural ones, blackfly season begins during the same period and lasts a few weeks.

- **What to wear:** You will need light clothing during this season, including shorts and T-shirts, but keep a sweater or light coat on hand for rainy days and cooler evenings.

- **What to do:** In some regions, you may want to install air conditioning in your home to beat the heat, or at least a fan to circulate air in your home. Better yet, get outside to enjoy Canada's lakes and wilderness. Camping is a common pastime for Canadians in the summer months. All you need is a tent, a few supplies, and an adventurous spirit!

### 2.2c   Autumn: September 21 to December 21

In autumn (or fall), days become noticeably shorter and the first frost appears. Leaves in many parts of the country turn from green to red, yellow, and brown before they fall from the trees. The weather during autumn can be rainy or dry; this is an unpredictable time of year. You can expect the first snow as early as September in some areas.

- **What to wear:** You will need a warm coat, gloves, hat, and boots as the end of autumn arrives and winter begins. Keep an umbrella handy.

- **What to do:** Autumn is a good time to start preparing your house for winter, such as cleaning the gutters. It's also a beautiful time of year to be outside to see the leaves changing colours.

### 2.2d   Winter: December 21 to March 21

You could see snow as early as September and as late as May in some areas, with daytime temperatures below zero degrees Celsius from December to mid-March and very cold nights. Winds can make temperatures feel even colder. The east and west coasts have milder winters, but snow and frost may still likely make an appearance, so you must be ready.

- **What to wear:** You must dress warmly to protect yourself from the cold when you are outside in winter. You will need a winter coat, mittens, hat, scarf, and boots with rubber soles. Wear multiple layers if possible. In the coldest regions, you may want to wear long underwear as well and make sure no skin is exposed to subfreezing temperatures. Children should be dressed particularly warm in snow pants, for example.

- **What to do:** Heating your home properly during this time of year becomes very important. Also, ensure you stay safe by shovelling snow from your driveway and adding salt to icy sidewalks. Driving can be treacherous in winter. Prepare your vehicle with proper snow tires and possibly chains if you plan on travelling to local mountains to partake in local winter activities such as skiing, sledding, or snowshoeing.

# 3. The People

Although Canada is a huge country, of its 34 million people, 80 percent live in towns and cities in the southern areas of the country. Most of Canada's population lives within 250 kilometres of the United States border.

Canada has 25 cities with populations of more than 100,000, but these account for less than 1 percent of Canada's landmass. Canada is only the 33rd largest country in the world in terms of population.

## 3.1 People in history

Canada is a multicultural society. Often called a "nation built by immigrants," the population of Canada is as diverse as its landscape.

The Aboriginal Peoples of Canada and Inuit in the Northern Territories were the original inhabitants of Canada, and are themselves made up of very diverse cultural and linguistic groups. They shared a similar way of living off the land, relying on hunting, fishing, gathering, and trading — and even warring with each other.

When the first European settlers came to Canada, primarily from Britain and France, they began trading with the Aboriginal Peoples. These settlers needed their help to explore, trade, and survive initially. However, they also battled with them, brought European diseases here that killed many, and eventually took the land away from them, starting a dark history for the native population that led to them being pushed onto reserve lands and into residential schools, and becoming subjects of the new Canadian government under the patriarchal *Indian Act*. Disputes still arise today about the Aboriginal Peoples' right to self-government, land entitlement, and much more.

Relations between the French and English were also troublesome. Considered the two founding nations of the country, they battled over land, trade, and religious differences. Today, there is still tension between the two, with Francophones dominating the province of Quebec, and Anglophones elsewhere. Over the years, there have been campaigns by Quebec nationalists to separate from Canada, but these attempts have been unsuccessful so far.

After the Dominion of Canada was officially formed in 1867, many immigrants from Britain and America came to settle in the growing country. Many Chinese migrants were brought over to help build the Canadian Pacific Railway that connected the two coasts of Canada by 1885. After the railway was completed, the Chinese were subject to discrimination including the Head Tax, a race-based entry fee. The Government of Canada apologized in 2006 for this discriminatory policy.

Immigrants from other countries such as Ukraine, Poland, Germany, Sweden, and Norway began to cross the ocean to the New World as well. Later, many European immigrants came to escape the wars and poverty on the continent. During the World Wars, the Canadian government interned immigrants from "enemy" countries, including Ukrainians during the First World War, and Japanese during the Second World War.

As Canada became a more progressive and modern society, and more and more immigrants from around the world came to the country for new opportunities and a new life, the Canadian government decided to define Canada as a "multicultural" society. Different from the so-called "melting pot" of the United States, Canada's notion of multiculturalism is one where people from many cultures, races, and religions can coexist in harmony.

## 3.2 Multiculturalism as official policy

Canada officially became a multicultural society in 1971 with the *Multiculturalism Act*, championed by the Prime Minister of the day, Pierre Elliot Trudeau. Canada became the first country in the world to declare multiculturalism as an official state policy. Today, multiculturalism is a symbol of Canada's national identity, but it's not without controversy. While statistics have shown that Canadians overall feel positive about diversity and immigration, there is also a desire for newcomers to integrate in terms of language and certain values, such as equality for women.

Canadian Multiculturalism Day is celebrated annually on June 27.

## 3.3 Equality under the law

Along with multiculturalism, Canada celebrates equality and freedom for all. The *Canadian Charter of Rights and Freedoms* protects your rights and freedoms in Canada, and sets out certain responsibilities as well. The Charter prohibits discrimination based on a person's ethnic origin, colour, religion, sex, age, and mental or physical disabilities.

Canadians believe in equality. Each person is equal before the law. Women and men have the same opportunity for education and success. Everyone has the right to participate in civil society and is encouraged to do so, from voting to running for political office.

## 3.4 Family life

Family life in Canada is as diverse as its people. While many families are made up of two parents with children, there are also a growing number of single-parent families and same-sex-parent families.

Canada has more than 1 million single-parent families, with women heading most. These women may be divorced, widowed, or never married. There are hundreds of thousands of step-families, created when adults who already have children marry one another. Many couples also choose not to get married and form common-law unions instead (unmarried people who live together in a committed relationship). After a certain time, common-law couples have similar legal rights to married couples.

Under Canadian law, marriage is a legal agreement between two people and may or may not have a religious significance. Each person in a marriage is viewed as an equal partner under law. Marriages between people of the same sex are also legal in Canada.

It is also common in Canada for two-parent families to have both parents working outside the home, while children attend daycare or are taken care of by caregivers, grandparents, or other family members.

Divorce is also a growing feature of family life in Canada. You do not have to be a Canadian citizen to divorce in Canada, and either partner can apply for a divorce. There are some residency requirements; for example, in Ontario a person has to reside there for one year before he or she can proceed with a divorce.

# 4. The Languages

Canada has two official languages: English and French. All Government of Canada services and documents are available in both of these languages.

There are also many unofficial languages. For example, the government websites for the Northwest Territories, Nunavut, and Yukon have options for French, English, and Inuktitut. There are also many Aboriginal dialects spoken across Canada, for example, Blackfoot and Cree.

English is the most common language spoken in all provinces except Quebec. In Quebec and in some parts of New Brunswick and Ontario, French is the more common language. Wherever you choose to settle, it's imperative that as a newcomer you learn one of the two official languages.

Fluency in English or French is critical to successful labour outcomes for immigrants. If you are reading this in your home country and have applied for your visa, please spend your waiting time upgrading your language skills. Many studies have confirmed that the most significant factor to successful establishment for newcomers to Canada is fluency in the language. This applies to all family members and not just the principal applicant.

Speaking English or French is extremely important to starting a life in Canada. Knowing one of these languages will help you take part in your new community, find a job, and talk to your children in the language they are learning at school and get to know their teachers. When you apply to become a Canadian citizen, you must demonstrate your knowledge of English or French.

There are government-funded English as a Second Language (ESL) programs available to immigrants, which are free to you after you arrive. Take advantage of these ESL programs, which may be referred to as Language Instruction for Newcomers to Canada (LINC) program or English Language Services for Adults (ELSA) or French as a Second Language (FSL).

Learning English or French is critical to your successful settlement in Canada. Better yet, start learning the language before you leave your homeland, and encourage all family members to do the same.

After you complete the basic levels of ESL or FSL, keep going and improve your English or French by taking classes at local colleges, community centres, and immigrant settlement agencies. Having your language skills assessed before you move to Canada can be helpful. A completed language assessment will determine how much, if any, language training you or your family members will need. There are several international assessment services that you can contact from your home country:

- International English Language Testing System (IELTS) is offered throughout the world.

- Canadian English Language Proficiency Index Program (CELPIP) Exam is offered to those who are in Canada.

- French language assessment is offered internationally; there is the Test d'évaluation de Français (TEF).

Ensure you are taking the appropriate language test for the immigration category under which you are applying.

# 5. Government and the Law

Canada is a democracy. Canadians value their right to vote and to decide who will govern their country. This means Canadian citizens have many rights — and the power to influence laws and the way governments at all levels work. Canadians do this by electing people to act on their behalf at the federal, provincial, territorial, and municipal levels. These representatives form the government.

## 5.1 Federal government

In Canada, the federal government is responsible for national matters such as defence, foreign policy, the Canadian postal service, international trade, matters of criminal law, employment insurance, income tax, and immigration and citizenship.

The federal government has three branches:

- **Executive branch:** Includes the Governor General, who is the Queen's representative in Canada; the Cabinet, which includes the elected Prime Minister and ministers responsible for specific portfolios; and government departments.

- **Legislative branch:** Includes the Governor General, the House of Commons, and the Senate. The House of Commons (or Lower House) is composed of 308 Members of Parliament (MPs) who are elected during federal elections to represent each federal riding in Canada. They propose, debate, and vote on legislation. The Senate (or Upper House) is made up of 105 senators appointed by the Governor General, on the advice of the Prime Minister. They review and suggest changes to any proposed new law.

- **Judicial branch:** Includes judges and the courts.

## 5.2 Provincial and territorial governments

Canada has ten provincial and three territorial governments. Canadians elect new provincial and territorial governments at least every five years. The elected leader of a territorial government is called the "Government Leader," while the elected leader of a provincial government is called the "Premier."

Provincial and territorial governments are responsible for many important government-regulated activities, including education. Provincial and territorial governments share responsibility with the federal government for health services, immigration, farming, social assistance, transportation, and environment.

While municipalities (cities and towns) have governments of their own that look after a good deal of day-to-day government work in Canada, they are overseen by the provinces and territories.

## 5.3 Municipal governments

Municipal governments run cities and towns. They have many responsibilities that affect the everyday lives of Canada's people, including firefighting, policing, snow removal, public transportation, community services, collecting property taxes, and more.

Municipal governments are made up of elected council members and a mayor. Local or municipal elections are held every two to four years, depending on the province or territory where the municipality is located.

## 5.4 Laws of the land

Canada is governed by a system of laws that apply to all people, including the police, judges, political leaders, and those who work for the government. The system of laws is called the "justice system." Everyone in Canada, whether they are a citizen or a permanent resident, is equal under the justice system. In Canada, women can have the same jobs as men and all the same responsibilities. People in Canada are not given better jobs because of their name, the amount of money they have, their social class, or their gender.

Some important laws to note include:

- Children younger than 12 years of age cannot be left at home alone or to care for younger children.

- All children aged 6 to 16 must receive some form of education.

- Depending on which part of Canada you live in, you must be either 18 or 19 years old to buy and drink alcohol.

- It is against the law to use, buy, or sell nonprescription drugs such as marijuana, heroin, and cocaine.

- It is against the law to make any kind of sexual remarks or advances if the other person is not receptive.

- It is against the law to hit or abuse anyone, including your spouse and children, either in the home or in public.

If you break a law in Canada and the justice system finds you guilty, there will be consequences. For minor offences such as theft or dangerous driving, you may have to pay fines, do community service, or spend a short time in prison. For more serious offences, such as hurting someone, you may go to prison for a longer time. For serious offences, such as killing someone, you may go to prison for life.

Being convicted of a crime may lead to the loss of your permanent resident status, your eligibility to become a citizen of Canada, or your ability to sponsor family members.

## 5.5 Policing

Canadian police help keep people safe and make sure they follow the law. You can ask the police for help in all kinds of situations, for example, if there has been an accident, if someone has stolen something from you, if someone has hurt you, if you see a crime taking place, or if someone you know has gone missing.

In Canada, federal and provincial governments share law enforcement. The Royal Canadian Mounted Police (RCMP) enforce federal laws across Canada. They also enforce provincial and territorial laws in all provinces except Ontario and Quebec. These two provinces have their own provincial police forces. Some municipalities in Canada have their own police forces to help enforce laws.

Cooperate with the police if you are stopped or questioned, and be ready to show some kind of identification. If the police arrest you, you have the right to know why and to have a lawyer and a translator, if you need one. Do not try to bribe police officers by offering money, gifts, or services. Under Canadian law, bribing a police officer is a serious crime.

The police are here to help you. If you are in an emergency, call 911 or 0 on your telephone and ask the operator to contact the police for you.

## 6. Human Rights

The *Canadian Charter of Rights and Freedoms* is part of Canada's Constitution and protects you from the moment you arrive in Canada. It sets out the values that Canadians live by and describes the kinds of personal human rights and freedoms you can expect in this country. Some of those rights and freedoms include the following:

- The right to life, liberty, and personal security.

- Freedom of conscience and religion.

- Freedom of thought, belief, opinion, and expression, including freedom of the press and other media.

- Freedom to hold peaceful meetings.

- Freedom to join groups.

- Protection from unreasonable search or seizure, and unjustified detainment and imprisonment.

- The right to be presumed innocent until proven guilty.

- The right to retain and instruct counsel (a lawyer) without delay.

- The right to a fair trial, through due process of law.

- The right to equal protection and benefit under the law, without discrimination.

Citizens of Canada have additional rights and freedoms such as the right to vote in elections.

Canadians are also encouraged to become informed about politics and help to improve their communities and the country through civic engagement.

Along with all these rights come responsibilities. People who live in Canada are expected to understand and obey Canadian laws, allow other Canadians to enjoy their rights and freedoms, and help preserve Canada's multicultural heritage.

It's important to note that Canada does not tolerate any form of abuse. Violence toward any person — man, woman, and child — is against the law. No one has the right to hit or threaten people or to force them into sexual activities. The law applies no matter who the person is.

Parents are required by law to take proper care of their children, and guardians of the sick or elderly must take proper care of those in their care. Police, doctors, teachers, and others will act if they suspect a child, spouse, or sick or elderly person is being abused. In serious cases of abuse, officials may take away children in danger or help a spouse or sick or elderly person escape the situation.

By law, parents in Canada must provide their children with the things they need to be healthy in their lives until they reach age 16. It is against the law in Canada to abuse children, be it physically, psychologically, or sexually. This can include spanking children enough to cause bruises, terrorizing or humiliating them, any kind of sexual contact, and neglect.

# 7. Education System

In Canada, the government provides an education for every child, in every province and territory, free of charge. The school year typically runs from September to June, five days a week. Public education (from kindergarten to Grade 12 — elementary to secondary school) is paid for through taxes and controlled by the provinces and territories. However, you will likely be asked to buy or provide some school supplies, (e.g., pens, notebooks).

Public education starts at age four or five, depending on the province or territory in which a child lives. The law states that children must receive an education until age 15 or 16, depending on where they live.

If your children do not speak English, they will attend English as a Second Language (ESL) program within the school environment. In Quebec, they will learn French.

It is important that you arrive in Canada with documents that will help schools place your child in the proper learning environment. Bring transcripts, report cards, samples of schoolwork, course outlines, and anything else that will help Canadian educators assess your child's level of learning.

There are also private school options that offer specialized education for annual tuition fees.

## 7.1 Postsecondary education

Many people in Canada further their studies with a postsecondary education (i.e., university, college, or trades program), which is the education they receive after they graduate from high school.

This is not free to students, and acceptance to a university or college is not guaranteed. Students must apply to the school of their choice and be prepared to pay tuition fees. While some academic and athletic scholarships and bursaries are available, most students must pay for tuition, often with the help of student loans.

# 8. Health-Care System

Canada is known worldwide for its health-care system. It is set up to respond to people's need for health care rather than their ability to pay for it. Often referred to as Medicare, the system is designed to make sure that all residents of Canada have reasonable access to health care from doctors and hospitals.

Instead of having a single national plan, Canada's health-care program is made up of provincial and territorial health-insurance plans, all of which share certain common features and standards.

## 8.1 Health insurance

All Canadians and permanent residents may apply for health insurance. When you have health insurance, you do not have to pay directly for most health-care services. Medical services are generally paid for through your taxes, while in some provinces you also have to pay a monthly insurance premium. Some employers may pay for medical premiums on your behalf.

When you use health-care services, such as visit a doctor or go to a hospital emergency, you simply show your health-insurance card to the hospital or medical clinic. Other health-care services, such as dental, chiropractic, and optometry services are not covered by the health-care system, and you must pay for these services or arrange for private or employer extended health-benefit insurance.

Be aware that in many provinces, including Ontario and British Columbia, there is a three-month waiting period before you will be eligible for regular health-care insurance coverage. Apply immediately after landing in Canada, but while you wait, ensure you are covered with private health insurance, such as Blue Cross, in case you need medical or emergency care.

Find out more about health insurance and how to apply for it on the Government of Canada's website (www.cic.gc.ca/english/newcomers/after-health.asp).

# 9. Social Assistance System

Canada also provides various types of social assistance to Canadians.

## 9.1 Old Age Security

The Old Age Security (OAS) pension is a monthly benefit available to most Canadians 65 years of age or older who have lived in Canada for at least ten years.

Canada has international social security agreements with many countries. People who have lived or worked in countries with which Canada has an agreement may qualify for OAS after as little as one year. See the Service Canada website for more information (www.servicecanada.gc.ca).

People who have low incomes and who receive OAS may also be able to receive the Guaranteed Income Supplement (GIS). If their spouses or widows are between 60 and 64 years of age, these people may also qualify for an Allowance or Allowance for the Survivor.

## 9.2   Canada Pension Plan

The Canada Pension Plan (CPP) retirement pension is a monthly benefit paid to people who have contributed to the CPP. All workers and employers in Canada pay into the CPP.

Canada has international social security agreements with many countries. If you have not lived and worked in Canada long enough to receive a Canadian pension, these agreements can allow Canada to count your pension credits from your home country to help you qualify for a pension.

# 10.  Economy and Labour Market

The Canadian economy was originally built on natural resources, such as forestry, agriculture, fisheries, and mining. Later, manufacturing and the financial industry grew in the east, while the west became better known for the oil industry in Alberta, and information technology in British Columbia.

Because of a higher population in eastern cities such as Toronto and Montreal, large companies are typically headquartered in those cities, and as a result so are many jobs. The Federal government job centre is largely in Ottawa, near Parliament.

Finding a job is more challenging for immigrants as they will need to prove that their credentials match the current requirements of the Canadian labour market. This process isn't always easy, and it often involves additional costs.

Some jobs in Canada are regulated (e.g., health care, law, engineering, financial services, and certain trades), and job applicants must have a licence, a certificate, or be registered with the regulatory body of the province or territory where they reside. This may involve taking an exam, undergoing a language assessment, doing supervised work practice, and paying certain fees, depending on the situation. Furthermore, full proficiency in either English or French will be vital, as it will greatly enhance your employability.

Other jobs are not regulated, but are still subject to some general expectations in terms of qualifications. In this case, it is up to the employer to assess an applicant's qualifications and to decide if he or she is a good match.

What an applicant can do is provide as much information as possible about his or her work and educational background. It is very important for immigrants to bring with them all the documents that might help them prove their qualifications: certificates, diplomas, reference letters from employers, awards, descriptions of work and study programs, grade transcripts, and performance reviews. The documents should be translated into English, French, or both, by an authorized translator.

The Foreign Credentials Referral Office (FCRO) is an office of Citizenship and Immigration Canada (CIC) that aims to assist immigrants with credential recognition. It has branches all across the country and it can provide some valuable tools to help newcomers navigate through the requirements of the local labour market. Immigrants can get a personalized report that can inform them of job descriptions, wages, necessary skills, education, and job opportunities in their desired profession. See the Government of Canada's website for more information (www.credentials.gc.ca).

Future immigrants can often apply for a licence or certificate even before leaving their country. Contact the regulatory body for your profession in the province or territory where you wish to settle and ask for assistance on the steps you have to take. You can avoid significant delays by starting a year in advance.

# 16
## Your First Steps in Canada

After you arrive, you will be faced with numerous tasks and challenges as you begin your journey in Canada. There will be moments when you will be confused and overwhelmed, but you should know that you can easily find ways to get guidance and support. Remember that 250,000 other immigrants go through the exact same things as you each year; if they can do it, so can you!

## 1. Ask for Help

There are many programs and organizations designed to serve new immigrants. You should take advantage of their services in order to speed up your integration, make friends, and maximize your chances of finding employment.

Your first step would be to contact an immigrant services organization. They can help you find a place to live, enroll your child in school, find a family doctor, look for a job, get language training, and access other services and programs for immigrants.

If you wish, your immigrant services organization can enroll you in a host program, where you are matched with a Canadian person or family who can help you practice your language skills, participate in community activities, and get a better knowledge of your city.

## 2.  Get Language Training

Knowing English (or French in some parts of Canada) is one of the most important aspects of settling successfully in Canada. If you need language training, there are free English as a Second Language (ESL) and French as a Second Language (FSL) courses available to newcomers.

Free ESL courses are often referred to as Language Instruction for Newcomers to Canada (LINC) or English Language Services for Adults (ELSA). Funded by the government and offered through immigrant services organizations, they offer free training for immigrants who need basic English or French. They have flexible study schedules and you can even get transportation and child minding.

Enhanced Language Training(ELT) addresses newcomers who need a higher level of English or French and job-specific language training. They also provide mentoring, cultural orientation classes, preparation for licensure exams, and work placement.

Without learning the languages of Canada (i.e., English or French), you will face isolation and increased challenges. Practice English or French as much as you can, by reading and talking to native speakers. Make a point to speak English or French for at least six hours a day, if you want dramatic improvement in a short time. Go to free ESL or FSL classes, get a tutor (there are many Canadian students who provide language classes for a reasonable price), watch Canadian television, or listen to the radio in English or French and repeat the words. Don't discard the old-fashioned way of using a grammar book and doing exercises. Language is your first ticket to success, and everything else depends on it.

## 3.  Find a Place to Rent

Finding a good place to rent in a new city can be very stressful, especially if you are staying at a hotel and don't want to spend too much on temporary accommodation. You can rent an apartment by the month, but most places will ask for a lease of at least six months.

The best place to search for a rental is in the local newspaper or on the Internet on sites such as craigslist.org or kijiji.ca. Most ads will have photos and detailed descriptions of the living conditions. You could also buy a public transit day pass and visit various residential neighbourhoods where you will likely see posters in front of some apartment buildings advertising rentals. If you like the location, you can call the number on the poster and set up an appointment with the building manager.

> **Note:** There are many unscrupulous people who prey on others. If you are unsure of a situation, go with your instincts and move on to the next rental. You can check the Better Business Bureau for reviews of apartment management companies.

There are many types of rentals: apartments, houses, condominiums (condos), shared housing, co-ops, and low-income housing. Most newcomers rent an apartment as their first home in Canada. Some apartment buildings have a gym, a pool, underground parking, a courtyard, and shared laundry facilities. Most apartments for rent are empty, but some buildings offer furnished apartments as well (usually short-term rentals). You have to keep the furnishings in the same condition as they were at the time you rented the place. Condominiums are privately owned apartments and are likely to cost more and have better living conditions.

Renting a house can be a good option if you have a large family, but you should expect the rent to be higher. You can also rent a suite in a house. If you are single, sharing rent can be a good way to save money and meet new people.

Low-cost housing is subsidized by the provincial government, but there is usually a waiting list, and sometimes this option is available only to those who have been in Canada for at least one year. You can check with BC Housing (www.bchousing.org) and the Ontario Ministry of Municipal Affairs and Housing (www.mah.gov.on.ca) to see what the requirements are.

Don't be shy to ask questions about the safety of various locations. Ask the hotel staff, the building managers — you can even strike up conversations with random people at coffee shops or on the bus. When visiting an apartment building, ask if it has security at night, if the hallways have video surveillance, and if the road to the nearest public transit connection is well lit. Check the locks at the doors and windows to see if they are in proper condition; if they are broken, it's a big red flag that the building is poorly managed. You can also find information on the Internet about the crime levels in various neighbourhoods.

Keep in mind that you have the right to ask any questions you think are necessary and that no one can pressure you into renting a home you don't like. Also, know that you cannot be denied a rental based on your ethnicity, colour, creed, gender, age, or disability.

If you are not planning to buy a vehicle right away, it is very important to be close to public transit and to be able to walk home safely from the nearest bus stop or subway station.

Check how close you are to grocery stores, multicultural centres, and schools (if you have children). Some neighbourhoods may look great, but can be difficult to live there without a vehicle.

Calculate what other costs you will have to pay in addition to your rent. Some buildings offer the water and heating included in the cost of the rent, but you will still have to pay for other utilities such as electricity, cable, Internet, parking, storage and other facilities, depending on the situation.

Ask what the consequences are in case you wish to move out before your lease expires. Do you have to pay a penalty, or is it enough to give a notice and, if so, how far in advance?

Make sure you understand the building rules. Many buildings do not allow pets or smoking inside the apartments, and some have strict policies regarding visitors and parties.

Once you have decided on a place to rent, you will have to sign a rental agreement. Read it carefully before you sign it and make sure you understand all the terms. If you are not confident in your language abilities, you can ask for help from an immigrant services organization.

Many buildings ask for a damage or security deposit when you first move in, which can be half the cost of a month's rent or more. When you move out, the security deposit will be returned to you, if you have not caused any significant damage to the premises. Ask what changes you are allowed to make inside the home (e.g., repainting, changing the carpets, installing certain appliances) and how that affects your security deposit.

In some provinces, such as Ontario, it is illegal to ask a tenant for a security deposit. However, owners in Ontario can ask a new tenant to pay what is called "last month's rent," but they must pay you back yearly interest for the sum and they cannot use it to compensate for damages.

If you plan to make a serious investment in furnishing your apartment, it is a good idea to purchase household insurance from a private company in case of fire or theft.

## 4. Buy a Home

Few people are lucky enough to be able to pay for a house in cash. This means that if you want to buy a house, you will have to get a mortgage. In order to do so, you have to give yourself a couple of years to establish a credit history in Canada. In this time, you can study the real estate market and the locations you like and plan your future investment in detail. Don't think only of the cost of the house itself; take into account the legal fees, maintenance, insurance, and property tax.

If you are ready to buy a house, take some time to check if the location is convenient and safe, if the property has all the features you need, has a good resale value, and is in good condition. You can hire an independent home inspector to check for hidden problems. Many sellers and real estate agents use strategies such as home staging (i.e., arranging the house and yard in an appealing way), sometimes to distract the buyer from certain serious flaws the property might have. A professional inspector can see through such marketing tricks and point out the real issues of the home. This can prevent you from making a bad investment, or it can help you negotiate a better price.

Before you start negotiating, it is best to get a credit check, speak to a financial adviser, and secure a pre-approved mortgage. You want to know what you can afford and make sure that your mortgage will not be more than 30 percent of your income.

## 5. Apply for a Social Insurance Number

Without a Social Insurance Number (SIN), you will not be able to get a job, open a bank account, or obtain your tax credits. You should apply for it within a few days of arriving in Canada. You will receive a card with the SIN number on it. Take good care of it and do not give away your SIN number unless it is necessary (i.e., when getting a job, opening a bank account, or applying for credit).

To apply, go to your nearest Service Canada centre (www.service canada.gc.ca). If your SIN card gets lost or stolen, to avoid identity theft, contact Service Canada immediately. Do not carry your SIN card with you (or your birth certificate or passport), unless you need it for a specific purpose.

# 6. Start Your Job Search

You will need a telephone number, especially when you start looking for a job. You can buy a cell phone on a monthly plan or with prepaid credit, and you can also have a landline installed. Telephone companies often offer bundles with telephone and Internet at a lower price than if you purchase them separately. It's important to have easy access to the Internet as you begin your job search, so having a small computer at home with Internet access is ideal.

Looking for a job in Canada may not be as easy as you imagined. There are many barriers that newcomers face, including a lack of "Canadian experience," a lack of understanding of Canadian corporate culture, poor language skills, a lack of appropriate soft skills in addition to technical skills, and more.

One of the most important things you will need to do is create a Canadianized résumé. There are many free workshops through immigrant services organizations that can help you not only create a résumé and cover letter, but better understand other job search strategies, including networking, mentoring, retraining, and having your foreign credentials assessed.

If you're in a licensed profession such as a nurse, engineer, or doctor, finding a job takes a backseat to getting your Canadian licence to practice. Such professions are regulated by individual licensing boards in each province and territory. A great online tool provided by the Government of Canada is the Job Bank, also known as "Working in Canada," which can help you find the appropriate board for your profession (http://www.jobbank.gc.ca/home-eng.do?lang=eng). You can also refer to Nick Noorani's website, Prepare for Canada (http://www.prepareforcanada.com/category/career-pathways/).

# 7. Apply for Health Care

One of the first things you should do when you arrive in Canada is apply for a health-insurance card. This way, you will not have to pay directly for most health- care services. You will pay for the services through your taxes and, in some provinces, through a monthly premium. Each family member needs to have their own health-care card.

In most provinces, newcomers have to wait three months to receive their health card, starting from the date their application is received. Until you receive the card, you can purchase temporary health insurance from a private company. Refugee claimants and refugees in need can access emergency and essential health-care services, which are covered by the Interim Federal Health Program.

You can find the health card applications forms at the following places:

- Doctor's office.

- Immigrant services organizations.

- Hospitals.

- Pharmacies.

- Provincial ministry responsible for health.

After you receive your health card, you should find a family doctor. You can ask for a list of local family doctors at your immigrant services organization, you can find them in the Yellow Pages, or you can walk into a family doctor's office and ask if it receives new patients. Most will not be accepting new regular patients as there is a shortage of family doctors in Canada.

If you need health care and you have not found a doctor yet, or if you cannot wait for an appointment with your family doctor, you can go to a walk-in clinic. Such clinics offer services for minor emergencies without an appointment and some are even open during evenings and weekends. You can find them in the Yellow Pages, under "Clinics." Also, you can get help for emergencies at your local hospital.

In Canada, children have to be immunized against certain infectious diseases. You should discuss this with your doctor and see if your family members have had all the required vaccines. You may need to provide a vaccination record to your children's school when you register them.

If you were told, during the medical exam you underwent for your residence application, that you need a follow-up exam when you arrive in Canada, you must report by telephone to the local health authority within 30 days of arriving. This happens when an applicant has an inactive infectious disease. The number of local health authorities can be found in the Blue Pages of the telephone book.

If you are pregnant, you should know that all working mothers in Canada have the right to maternity leave. If you need more information about this, contact a Service Canada centre or your local provincial or territorial ministry responsible for labour. Also, you can get valuable prenatal and postnatal guidance from your local hospital or community service centre.

## 8. Emergency Services

In most Canadian cities, the emergency number is 911. You can call this number, or go to the emergency room of your local hospital. If your community does not have 911 services, dial 0 and ask the operator for help.

If you call 911, you will reach an operator who will ask you a few questions and then send you the appropriate help (i.e., paramedics, ambulance, fire department, police). Be prepared to give your address and describe the type of emergency and the condition of the injured person. It is crucial to stay as calm as possible; the sooner you give the operator all the needed information, the sooner you will get assistance. Follow the operator's instructions and wait for help to arrive.

Many people keep emergency lists next to their telephone, or add emergency numbers in the telephone memory.

If you have allergies, diabetes, high blood pressure, or any other serious medical conditions, ask your doctor about MedicAlert tags or bracelets (www.medicalert.ca). In case of a medical emergency, MedicAlert will help doctors in giving you the right treatment.

## 9. Enroll Your Children in School

You can register your child at the local school or at the local school board office. To find the local school board, ask your immigrant services organization or access the website of the Ministry of Education in your province or territory.

When you register your child, you must bring the following documents:

- Permanent Resident Card, Record of Landing (IMM 1000), or Confirmation of Permanent Residence (IMM 5292).

- Child's birth certificate.

- Child's vaccination records.

- Child's previous school records, translated into English or French.

Your child may get tested on mathematics and language so that he or she can be placed in the right grade. If the school decides that the child needs additional language training, he or she may be placed in an English as a Second Language (ESL) class.

If the school is not easily accessible by walking or public transit, your child may be able to travel to class in a bus provided by the school, for free or at a very low cost.

For higher education, contact the college or university of your choice and ask for details. If you haven't decided on one, you can ask for advice at your immigrant services organization.

## 10. Open a Bank Account and Get Credit

It is recommended to open a bank account soon after you arrive in Canada. Opening an account is free, but there may be a cost to maintain it. When you get a job, you can ask your employer to deposit your salary directly into your bank account.

When choosing a bank, take into account its services, fees, hours of operation, and location. Meet with a bank representative and discuss what type of account would be best for you. You will have to bring identification and provide proof of where you live (you can bring your rental agreement or a bill). You can ask to have access to online banking. It will make it easier to pay your bills and check your bank balance.

Getting a credit card is very useful. It will help you establish a credit history and make online payments. However, without a job and an existing credit history, you will, most likely, be required to leave a deposit for a minimum of one year. You can also get a credit card at some stores. Establishing a credit history is very important because you will need it when you want to obtain a mortgage or another type of loan. Your credit history will be recorded by one of the three major credit bureaus: Equifax, Experian, or TransUnion. Every time you use your credit, the information will be sent to these bureaus. You are entitled to get free reports of your credit history; just contact each of the three bureaus and ask for a copy of your credit report.

## 11. Get Around on Transit

To use public transit, you will have to purchase tickets or a monthly pass. You can purchase tickets in advance, in groups of ten, or you can pay as you travel. Keep in mind that you will need exact change when buying a ticket on the bus. If you bought tickets in advance, you still need to validate them when you board the bus. On the back of the ticket, the machine will print the period for which it is valid (usually 90 minutes); during this period, you can use the same ticket to board different buses, or to switch from the bus to subway.

In larger cities areas are divided into different zones so the ticket prices may differ depending on whether you travel within one zone or across zones. If you have a one-zone ticket and wish to travel to another zone, you will be asked to pay the price difference when boarding the bus.

Bus stops will have panels showing which buses stop there and their destination. Many bus stops will also post the transit schedules. If you want to know the schedule of a certain bus or how to get from one place to another, you can access the website of your local transit company.

## 12. Driving in Canada

While you may be able to use your foreign driver's licence for the first few months in Canada, you will, eventually, have to get a Canadian licence. Contact your local motor vehicle licensing agency to learn how to get licensed. You will have to carry your licence with you whenever you drive, together with the vehicle's registration and insurance.

All vehicles in Canada must be insured. The insurance costs will vary according to the type of vehicle you drive and your driving record.

You will need to take a road test and a knowledge test on driving rules. Road safety is extremely important. Make sure you learn Canadian traffic safety rules very well, to avoid accidents, fines, high insurance costs, or the loss of your licence. You may even consider getting a few private driving lessons, especially if you haven't driven in a long time.

Here are a few tips on Canadian traffic safety:

- Take into account the weather.

- Stay within the posted speed limits.

- Never drink and drive.

- Respect emergency vehicles (pull to the side of the road when police cars, fire trucks, and ambulances need to pass and slow down when they are parked on the side of the road with their lights flashing).

- Wear your seatbelt.

- Yield to school buses; stop when you see red lights flashing on a school bus — this means that children are getting on or off the bus and they may be crossing the street.

- Use appropriate infant and child car seats.

- Respect parking signs.

- Never ever leave the scene of an accident. Call the police to report the accident, request an ambulance (if necessary), and exchange insurance information with the other driver.

# 13. Protect Your Identity

Identity theft is a very serious, and, unfortunately, very common crime. A criminal who has access to your personal information can use it to buy goods at your expense, open bank accounts in your name, and even get credit that you will have to pay back. Keep your identification papers in a safe place and do not lend them to anyone. If you need them, see if you can use copies instead of the originals. If any identification documents get lost or stolen, report them immediately and ask for replacements.

You should also be careful with what you throw away (e.g., bank statements, credit card bills, pre-approved credit card applications) because identity thieves use local dumps to fish for information. Use a shredder to get rid of such documents once you don't need them anymore. If your credit cards get lost or stolen, call your bank or credit card company and cancel them immediately.

# 14. Apply for Benefits

It's no one's ideal scenario, but if your income is not enough to cover the needs of your family, you can apply for assistance until the situation improves.

Families with children younger than 18 can apply for the Canada Child Tax benefit. This is a monthly tax-free payment and it is based on factors such as the number of children you have, their ages, your income, and your province or territory of residence. To obtain the Canada Child Tax benefit, you need to file an income tax return each year. If you haven't been in Canada long enough to file a tax return, you need to file a separate form to declare your world income. You will have to provide proof of your immigration status and proof of birth for any of your children born outside Canada.

Another option for families with modest incomes is applying for the GST/HST credit. This credit helps you offset all or part of the Goods and Services Tax (GST) or Harmonized Sales Tax (HST) that you pay. To be eligible, you have to be older than 19 and a resident of Canada; if you are younger than 19, you need to be a parent or to have a spouse or common-law partner. You can get the Credit Application for Individuals Who become Residents of Canada (Form RC151) for the GST/HST credit by calling the Canada Revenue Agency or visiting the website (www.cra.gc.ca).

Also, take advantage of the various programs offered to the unemployed or underemployed. They can help steer your career on the right path, and can give you valuable opportunities to network.

# 17
## Cost of Living in Canada

The cost of living can vary greatly from one Canadian city to another. The most significant variable is for housing (i.e., rent or mortgage payments), which is the biggest monthly expense you will have.

## 1. Renting or Buying a Home

Typical rent for a bachelor apartment can go from $700 to $2,000 in a big city and from $500 to $800 in a small town, depending on the location and living conditions. Many apartment complexes include utilities such as water and heat in the price of the rent, while electricity, cable, and phone bills are your responsibility. An average electricity cost would be around $80 per month.

Most rental apartment buildings require a lease for a minimum of six months and a security deposit, which is normally half the monthly rent. Also, they often do not take cash or credit. You can pay with a cheque, debit card, or money order.

Downtown rents tend to be more expensive due to the convenient central location. Outlying areas often have more affordable rents and better living standards (e.g., bigger apartments, more parks and playgrounds, and inexpensive shopping venues), but longer commutes into the city.

In addition to a typical apartment rental, you may also be able to rent a private suite in a house, a whole house, town home, or a room in a house with a shared kitchen and bathroom. These rentals are typically offered by individual owners, rather than management companies, who handle most apartment complex rentals. There may be more flexibility if you rent from an individual, but you still have all the same tenant rights and responsibilities as any other renter. Each province and territory has its own tenancy rules and guidelines, which can be found on housing ministry websites.

If you decide to buy a house, things are more complicated and more expensive. Housing prices in Canada vary across the country, with the most expensive homes found in Greater Vancouver, followed by other big cities such as Toronto. The least expensive housing is found in the Prairies and northern parts of the country.

Most Canadians get a mortgage loan from a bank, which requires a substantial down payment.

Even with a down payment, in order to obtain a loan, you first need to establish a credit rating (which proves to the bank that you are able to pay back the loan). In most cases, immigrants have to wait a few years before they establish a good credit rating in Canada and can access a mortgage loan.

Other expenses related to owning a house are property tax and household insurance.

## 2. Food

On average, Canadians spend between $200 and $300 per person each month on groceries. Supermarkets have sales on various items all the time, and you will probably receive many flyers and coupons in your mailbox.

Farmers' markets are not very common in Canada, but a great variety of fresh fruits and vegetables are available year-round. Seasonal produce will cost less and have better flavour so take advantage of it while it lasts. Organic foods tend to be significantly more expensive and are usually sold in specialty stores or in special aisles at regular stores. In a big city, it is very likely that you will find at least one store or restaurant that caters to your ethnic community.

Dining out will definitely increase your food bill. Take some time to know your city before you start sampling the local restaurants.

Big Canadian cities have countless eating establishments, from fast food chains to fine dining, which can be very tempting, but it is a good idea to save restaurant outings for special occasions as they can get pricey and often are full of high-calorie, high-fat options.

# 3. Tipping

In Canada, it is customary to tip 15 to 25 percent on the bill for a variety of services. You do not have to do it, but the social pressure exists, and most people do tip. You may want to budget for it.

Professional categories that usually receive tips include: waiters, bartenders, hotel valets, room attendants, manicurists, hairdressers, beauticians, cab drivers, parking valets, bellhops, and porters.

It is not customary to tip retail associates or clerks, and you should never attempt to tip doctors, nurses, police, or people who work in public institutions. If you want to express your gratitude toward medical staff or public institution staff, you can simply send a "thank you" card.

# 4. Clothing

Your clothing expenses will depend greatly on your personal taste and standards. Still, you should know that Canadians tend to favour casual styles and do not tend to judge people by the labels they wear or by the value of their attire.

If saving money is your number one priority, you can definitely find clothing items for less than $10 and footwear for less than $30, especially in the discount bins at some stores. Avoid trendy shopping locations, and hunt for clearance sales as much as possible. You may also want to give thrift stores (i.e., secondhand stores) a chance.

If you have many valuable clothes and accessories (e.g., designer items) at home in your country of origin that will not fit into your luggage, it would be a good idea to pack them and have your family or friends ship them to you later. You don't know how long it will be until you can afford to do high-end shopping again, so why not make the most of what you already own?

Since you will be job hunting, you should know that the standard interview style in Canada is smart-casual (e.g., dress pants or skirt, and a buttoned shirt or a simple blouse, and blazer). Very few employers expect you to come to the interview in an elegant three-piece suit. Bring with you the things you will need the most, and save the elegant outfits for later.

# 5. Furniture

As with clothes, prices on furniture differ greatly from store to store. Beds and couches are particularly expensive so it may not be possible for you to buy new as soon as you get here. You can find used furniture at great prices at garage sales and thrift stores, or on websites such as Craigslist or Kijiji. Also, check the laundry room in your apartment building as soon as you move in: Often, people who move out want to get rid of some furniture and post ads for the other tenants.

Another option is to contact your local immigrant community centre or church to see if they have any available donations.

Obviously, finding suitable furniture takes a bit of time, you will not be able to get it all as soon as you move into your home. Many immigrants choose to sleep on inflatable mattresses (which cost between $30 and $150) for a short while, until they learn what their options are.

# 6. Appliances and Electronics

If you bring appliances and/or electronics from your country of origin, you may need to buy some adapters. Note that Canada uses 110 volts.

You can find basic appliances at very good prices. Some big stores carry small household appliances for less than $20 (e.g., toasters, mixers, blenders, coffeemakers, hair dryers, clothes irons), and larger ones for less than $70 (e.g., microwaves, vacuum cleaners).

Plasma or flat-screen television sets can cost anywhere from $200 to more than $2,000, depending on the size and brand. Classic television sets cost considerably less.

Laptops and desktop computers for average use can be quite expensive (from $500 to $1,300), but, if possible, it would be best to invest in one. Your job search will be highly dependent on the Internet, and you will also need it to find useful information fast (e.g., maps, routes, phone numbers, and services) and to keep in touch with your loved ones at home. By using Skype on your computer you can save hundreds of dollars on long-distance bills!

Multifunctional printers for home use can cost from $60 to more than $200. Employment centres usually offer free printing services to their clients (including basic business cards), and you will definitely have to print many résumés. Paying for copying, scanning, and printing is expensive so take advantage of any free services you can get, or buy your own printer.

When you buy electronics, dealers will try to sell you an extended warranty plan (for one or two years). The cost of this plan is usually 10 percent of the item cost. It is up to you to decide if you want it or not, but remember that each item has a manufacturer warranty that is included in the price. The advantage of the extended warranty plan is that you can take your item back to the store in case it breaks (instead of sending it to the manufacturer), and the store will fix it or give you a new one. The disadvantage is that you may not need it at all (e.g., few computers break in less than a year), or if you believe in "Murphy's Law," your item can break the day after your warranty expires. Savvy shoppers usually consider extended warranties to be unnecessary.

You will, most likely, have to purchase a Canadian cell phone. Some Canadian cell phones have SIM cards, some do not. Most cell phone carriers offer some phones for free or at a considerable discount if you sign up for a two- or three-year plan. If you find their offers confusing, you could simply buy a less expensive cell phone and prepaid airtime until you feel confident enough to commit to a contract. A cell phone plan costs around $40 per month, but you can also buy prepaid credit for as little as $10. You can choose the plan that is best for your needs. You can purchase inexpensive long-distance phone plans from specialized companies to make it easier to keep in touch with your loved ones at home.

Phone and Internet costs are, on average, $40 a month. Employment centres usually provide free Internet access, but it is a good idea to get your home connection because you will use the Internet extensively in your job search.

Basic cable costs around $30 to $40. For specialty channels, you will have to pay extra.

# 7. Transportation

Public transit is very good in most Canadian cities. Vancouver, Toronto, Calgary, Edmonton, Montreal, and Ottawa have rapid transit train systems.

During your first months in Canada, you will have to travel a lot so it would be best to purchase a monthly bus pass and not worry about always having exact change for a bus ticket. A monthly bus pass can cost between $70 and $150 depending on the areas it covers. An individual ticket can cost between $2.50 and $3.75. Transit companies offer discounts for children, students, and seniors 65 years or older.

Some newcomers decide to buy a vehicle, especially if they have small children. The law states that all vehicles must be insured so you must also take into account the insurance costs. Gas costs range from $1.15 to $1.50 per litre. If you are confident in your technical knowledge, you can buy a used vehicle directly from the vendor or through a used vehicle dealership.

Renting a car is expensive and it is best to save that for special situations. If you choose to rent, you are looking at a minimum of $900 per month.

Taxi services in Canada charge between $1 and $2 per kilometre, with a starting price of at least $3.

# 8. Health Care

As mentioned in the previous chapter, newcomers have to wait three months before they can get health insurance in several provinces. If you wish to be covered during these initial three months, you need to purchase insurance from a private company.

Once you're eligible for public health care, you may be faced with paying a monthly premium, depending on your province or territory. The costs of these public health-care premiums depend on the area you choose and the size of your family.

Dental care is very expensive in Canada. Dental insurance plans can be purchased from private companies and some employers offer dental plans to their employees. It is not covered by Canada's public health-care system. Other areas that are not covered in full or in part include optometry, chiropractic, physiotherapy, and psychological counselling.

## 9. Entertainment

The price of a ticket for a show, festival, concert or sports match depend on the type of the event and the seating, going from less than $10 to hundreds of dollars. Movie tickets cost between $7 to $15. Local libraries lend DVDs and CDs at no cost, and there are also many community theatres that provide free performances.

## 10. Other Expenses

Alcohol and cigarettes are expensive because the taxes on such items are very high. It is illegal to order cigarettes from other countries.

Postage within Canada, for a simple letter, is $0.85. International postage costs $2.50. Every January, stamp prices slightly increase. International parcels can be quite expensive depending on the size and mailing option.

The monthly cost of personal care and cleaning supplies should not be more than $30 per person, but this also depends on your personal preferences. Supermarkets have store brands of acceptable quality (many are just as good as big brand products), and there are also dollar stores where you can find a myriad of small household and personal-care items.

A simple haircut costs around $25 to $30 for men and somewhat higher for women.

Apartment buildings usually have laundry rooms, and you will be charged for each wash from $2.50 to $4. You can use coins or a laundry card that you will get from the building receptionist and that you can charge from your debit or credit card.

## 11. Taxes

When you get a job, the money deducted from your paycheque will be around 25 to 35 percent. This money is used to pay for things such as Employment Insurance (EI), pension plans, income taxes, and union dues (if applicable). The percentage may be higher than what you are accustomed to, but remember that Canadians enjoy a higher living standard, and such a standard needs to be supported by taxpayers.

Most goods and services you buy also have added sales taxes. These are the Goods and Services Tax (GST) and Provincial Sales Tax (PST). The GST is 5 percent, and the PST is between 7 and 10 percent, depending on the province.

Ontario, Newfoundland and Labrador, and Nova Scotia have a Harmonized Sales Tax (HST), which means they combine the GST and PST into one tax. BC has transitioned back from a recent change to HST.

Yukon, Northwest Territories, Nunavut, and Alberta do not have a Provincial Sales Tax.

# 18
## Settling In

Immigrating in search of a better life is a very brave decision. It shows that you are a person of action and a risk-taker and that you can take your life in your hands and change it to whatever you want it to be.

Many of those you leave behind will admire or envy your courage, and expect you to send them good news about your success very soon. Maybe you imagine the same thing: That your life will come together as soon as you set foot in the country of your dreams. Usually, all the focus and energy goes to the actual immigration process and moving preparation such as raising money, gathering the paperwork, selling properties, packing, and searching for convenient airfares. All is concentrated around the idea of the big leap.

Immigrating may be the big leap, but going through the first year after arriving to Canada is the big challenge. Unless you are among the very few who have immigrated more than once, you are in for an experience incomparable with anything you have ever dealt with before. You should embrace this experience, but also be prepared for the pitfalls of starting over in a new country.

# 1. An Emotional Journey

There are various stages of emotions that you will go through as you settle in Canada. The following sections will describe those stages and what you can do to combat the negativity.

Of course, not everybody experiences all these stages, or they don't happen in the same order. Nevertheless, you will feel the weight of this great challenge and you need to be prepared to deal with it.

## 1.1 The first stage

The initial stage after landing in Canada is often referred to as the "honeymoon phase." For the first month or so, many newcomers are still in "visitor mode"; they feel like tourists on holiday, exploring and enjoying all the interesting aspects of the new culture. Try to make the best out of this phase because you will need that infusion of optimism to help you cope with the actual adjustment.

## 1.2 The second stage

The second stage is usually full of extreme emotions, doubts, anxieties, homesickness, loneliness, and frustration. If you have language difficulties and few ties to your ethnic community, you may experience a deep feeling of isolation. You may also be tempted to compare Canada to your home country and point out everything you feel was better back home. To help you cope with your anxiety and confusion the following section will help you deal with these negative feelings.

### 1.2a Reach out

If you don't know anyone in Canada, go to an immigrant services organization or community centre. When you arrive at the airport, the immigration officer will give you a booklet with useful contacts, in which you will find all the addresses of the cultural community centres in your area.

### 1.2b Avoid comparisons

While it's very normal to miss home, realize that Canada will never be exactly like the country you left behind. Some of the good things you had at home may not be available here; no country is perfect. Focus on the positives.

### 1.2c  Manage your budget carefully

Shrinking savings are one of the major sources of panic for new immigrants. Avoid overspending in order to preserve your sense of security for as long as possible. Also, do not fall into the common trap of constantly comparing Canadian prices with the prices in your home country. "Back home this costs a lot less" — such a mindset can only put you in a pessimistic mood.

### 1.2d  Get involved

The best way to forget about your problems is to devote yourself to others. Volunteer at an organization or a cause that you feel could use your skills and knowledge. You will make friends, gain a sense of community, and learn new things. In Canada, volunteering counts as work experience that you can add to your résumé.

### 1.2e  Enjoy diversity

Few countries offer such a high level of diversity as Canada. There are plenty of ethnic festivals, restaurants, shops, and cultural centres where you can take part. In addition, you may discover that your culture has surprising similarities with other cultures from opposite ends of the world.

### 1.2f  Keep your expectations realistic

Success won't happen overnight. It is very unlikely that you will easily find a job that matches the status you had in your home country. It's no piece of cake even for Canadian-born citizens to reach a higher professional level. Accept that it takes time and that you may have to start low and work your way up.

All this being said, it is still normal to feel confused and scared occasionally. Acknowledge your feelings, but don't let them overwhelm you.

## 1.3  The third stage

The next stage of adapting to Canada is characterized by a higher level of confidence and comfort. You've probably made some friends, learned more about the job-search process, improved your language skills, discovered the best places to shop, and visited a few places; in other words, you start to feel more like you belong.

## 1.4 The fourth stage

Finally, the fourth stage is one of acceptance and contentment. Things may not yet be where you want them to be, but they are going in the right direction. You feel like you've started to build a life in Canada, and you develop a sense of attachment to certain places, values, or cultural aspects.

# 2. Canadian Culture and Expectations

By the time you get through these typical stages of settlement in Canada, you will have a much better understanding of Canadian culture and expectations. The following sections are a few important ones to note.

## 2.1 Dressing appropriately

Try to dress smart when going to job interviews or in the workplace. This doesn't necessarily mean a suit and tie, but you need to look polished. It is preferable to save ethnic wear for special occasions, or when you are at home or in your ethnic community.

Grooming well is also very important. Food and bodily odours can hinder your adaptation considerably.

One aspect that some foreigners find strange is that many places in Canada have a scent-free policy, meaning that they do not allow strong perfumes or colognes. This is because they can cause severe migraines and allergies for some people so it is best to avoid strong scents in the workplace or when going to classes or workshops. Also note many hospitals and medical clinics have adopted the scent-free policy.

## 2.2 Behaving politely

Canadians are known for being very polite and friendly. Smile and make eye contact when you talk to people. Handshakes should be short and firm. Kissing on the cheek is not customary in Canada, nor is kissing a woman's hand as a greeting.

Be friendly to people, but also be aware that relationships may be very different from those in your home country. Some countries have close-knit communities, while others place more value on privacy and discretion (especially in big cities).

"Thank you," "please," and "excuse me" are keywords when interacting with Canadians.

It is usually not acceptable to ask people you don't know well about their religion, political views, sexual mores, or financial problems. You don't want to come off as nosy or, worse, judgmental.

## 2.3 Respecting diversity

Many immigrants come from monoethnic cultures, but Canada is the exact opposite of that. People of all races, ethnicities, and creeds live here, so it's important to find ways to coexist in peace.

Do not pressure people to share aspects of their ethnicity or religion, no matter how curious you are. You may ask a polite question, but, if you see any reluctance, do not insist.

Also, avoid the common assumption that all visible minorities are foreign. Many have been here for generations and identify simply as Canadian. Do not ask questions like "Where are you from?" based solely on a person's race.

## 2.4 Women's issues

For women, adapting to life in Canada often involves worries about parenting, child care, and gender roles. There are special programs aimed at helping immigrant women adjust. Many of these programs offer free child care during their workshops and seminars. Whether you are married or a single woman, you can use such opportunities to make female friends who share your interests and can offer emotional support.

Canadian law supports equality between men and women, and protects women and children from domestic abuse. It is important to know your rights and the appropriate resources, such as women's shelters or support groups.

In the workplace, you are entitled to the same respect as your male colleagues. Sexual discrimination and sexual harassment are not acceptable and constitute serious offences in Canada.

## 2.5 Men's issues

For men, the biggest gender-related pressures come from the feeling of failure to provide for the family adequately in Canada, and sometimes from re-evaluating gender roles. Men are more likely to blame themselves for professional and financial hardships. If you have been the sole or main provider for your family in your home country, the pressure can be enormous.

While you take the necessary steps to adjust to a new and different labour market, try to see the silver lining: You have more time to spend with your family. Like everybody else, Canadians work hard and often wish they had more time to dedicate to family life. Take advantage of your free time and do the family activities you never had the chance to do back when you were working.

The egalitarian view on gender can sometimes be a source of confusion for new immigrants, but this is one aspect of Canadian society that is not negotiable. Women have the same rights as men, and they are protected from physical and emotional abuse by very strict laws.

Women bosses and work colleagues are respected in the same way as their male counterparts. It is not acceptable to make sexual or discriminatory remarks in the workplace; this can (and usually does) result in termination of the work contract.

## 2.6 Parenting issues

Immigrant children have their own obstacles to overcome. It is usually traumatic for children to be separated from their friends and schoolmates, sometimes from a boyfriend or girlfriend, and this can cause a lot of family drama at first.

The good news is that children are always the first to adapt. We are most flexible when we are young, and, before you know it, they will make new friends and start enjoying their life in Canada.

However, parents have to pay attention to their children's behaviour and mood, especially in the first months at a new school. Encourage your child to open up to you and tell you about any incidents of bullying, discrimination, and racism so that you can take the appropriate measures.

If your child is experiencing bullying, you should never try to take things into your own hands. Hitting or threatening another child can get you into serious trouble. Have a meeting with the school principal, or talk to the parents of the bully and ask them to put a stop to the child's behaviour.

Immigrant teenagers can have a hard time adapting, too. Worries about body image, clothing, and dating will be bigger than usual when moving to a new country. Encourage your teenagers to attend extracurricular activities such as joining different clubs or volunteering, in order for them to meet other youth and keep themselves busy. Also, taking a part-time job could give them a healthy sense of independence and control.

## 2.7 Seniors' issues

Seniors often immigrate to Canada when they already have children here, usually to give them a hand in raising their family. It is much harder for them to adjust; common issues are a sense of dependence on their children, loneliness, and language difficulties.

If you are a senior immigrant, it is beneficial for you to get out of the house and socialize. There are senior centres that offer all sorts of entertaining activities, which are a good opportunity to practice English or French. Settlement organizations also offer special services and guidance for seniors.

Avoid restricting your contacts to your ethnic community. Even if it is hard to get over the language barrier, meeting seniors from other cultures could open up new horizons for you. Learn about a new cuisine or craft, communicate with other grandparents when you take your grandchildren to the park, or take language classes.

## 2.8 Singles' issues

Being alone in a new country can be an overwhelming experience. Depression and loneliness are often experienced by the ones who come on their own, especially if they are alone during a birthday, a holiday, or another special occasion.

As always, the answer is to start socializing as soon as possible. Go to a community centre, volunteer, attend a job-hunting workshop, and look for people your age with whom you have things in common. Getting a roommate is a good way to feel less lonely and reducing your living expenses.

Dating in Canada may be different than what you know from your home country. Before looking for love, notice the societal norms when it comes to romance and sexuality. Wait until you build a support system of friends and acquaintances to avoid getting involved in a codependent relationship simply out of loneliness.

If you feel overwhelmed and depressed by the challenges of adapting to your new life, ask your family doctor to recommend the best ways to access mental health support. Regardless of what you may have learned in your home country, be reassured that it is in no way shameful to attend therapy in Canada.

# 19
# Maintaining Your Permanent Resident Status

Once you become a permanent resident, you have an obligation to maintain your residency status. A permanent resident is required to reside in Canada for two out of every five years, or 730 days within five years. Accordingly, when you first obtain your Permanent Resident Card, it will give you a five-year period to reside in Canada.

Many people come to Canada to become permanent residents first and then return to their home country to settle their affairs such as selling their house and finishing employment. The required two years of residency can be accumulated at any time within the five-year window of residency status granted with the issuance of your Permanent Resident Card also known as the "Maple Leaf Card." Keep in mind that you will have to prove that you meet the minimum time requirements, or that you will be able to meet them before the five years expire.

Some immigration officers are very probing in their questions about the time that persons have spent outside of Canada. It is not unusual for a determination to be made at the border that an individual has lost their permanent resident status because he or she has been out of the country for an extended period of time and he or she can no longer meet the two-year residency requirement for the balance of the validity of their Maple Leaf Card. Accordingly, it is advisable that you keep precise records of the time that you spend in and out of Canada so that you can always demonstrate that you have met the residency requirements.

There are some exceptions to the need to be "physically present" in Canada. You can live abroad if the following applies:

- You are accompanying a Canadian citizen that is your spouse, common-law partner, or parent (if you are younger than 19 years old).

- If you are employed full time by a Canadian company or public service, or assigned to work for a client of the Canadian company or public service abroad.

- If you are accompanying a permanent resident that is your spouse, common-law partner, or parent (if you are you are younger than 19 years old) who is employed full time by a Canadian company or public service.

In all of these cases, you will be required to provide supporting documentation of your work status or of your relationship to the person you are accompanying and his or her work status.

# 1. Renewing Your Permanent Resident Card

The Permanent Resident Card is only valid for a period of five years. Accordingly, unless you have become a citizen within that five-year period of time, it will be necessary for you to renew your Permanent Resident Card. As the renewal process can take many months, it is advisable to apply for renewal of your Permanent Resident Card at least six months prior to it expiring if not earlier than that.

If you have come to Canada as a permanent resident and stayed and lived permanently in Canada, it is advisable to apply for your citizenship as soon as possible so that you won't need to apply to renew your Permanent Resident Card every five years.

For Permanent Resident Card renewals and citizenship applications, you will need to show your Confirmation of Permanent Residence (COPR) document, your original passport with the stamp of entry to Canada, plus two pieces of identification.

## 2. Becoming a Citizen

The citizenship process is a lengthy application process and many people who have applied to obtain their citizenship also have had to apply to renew Permanent Resident Cards to allow them to travel internationally. Canada's citizenship laws have recently changed and as of mid-2015, you will need four years of Canadian residency rather than three to be eligible to apply for Canadian citizenship so you will most certainly need to renew your Permanent Resident Card while applying for citizenship. If your Permanent Resident Card has expired and you are travelling internationally and are originally from a country that requires a visa to enter Canada, you will need to apply for a travel document abroad in order to return to Canada while your renewal of Permanent Resident Card application is being finalized (http://www.cic.gc.ca/english/information/applications/travel.asp).

Obtaining citizenship eliminates the need to renew your Permanent Resident Card on a regular basis. Citizenship also entitles you to obtain a Canadian passport and confers other rights such as the right to vote in Canadian elections.

In order to be eligible to apply for Canadian citizenship, you must obtain four full years of physical presence in Canada within a six-year period. This means that you need to obtain 1,460 days of physical presence in Canada within a 2,190-day period. It is again recommended that you keep very precise records of your travel outside of Canada with supporting proof so that you can demonstrate that you have met the required number of days of physical presence in Canada to meet the citizenship requirement.

In the past, residency in Canada was not defined and there was not a physical presence standard. However, citizenship judges as well as Federal Court judges were interpreting the residency requirement very strictly and people who were merely a few days short of 1,095 days of physical presence in Canada often had their applications for citizenship rejected. Now physical presence in Canada is the legal standard to be eligible for Canadian citizenship.

Canada has no restrictions on dual citizenship, but you will need to meet all of the following criteria before you can be sworn in as a citizen:

- Demonstrate that you are able to speak, read, write, and understand either of Canada's two official languages, English or French.

- Be 18 years of age or older to apply on your own behalf.

- Be a permanent resident.

- Have knowledge of Canada, including its history, politics, and geography.

- Have lived in Canada for a total of four out of the six years preceding your application (if you are older than 18) and you must spend at least 183 days in Canada in each of those six years.

- Understand your rights and responsibilities as a Canadian citizen.

- Be prepared to take an oath (or affirmation) of citizenship.

With Canadian citizenship comes many privileges as well as many responsibilities. As a citizen you will be entitled to the following:

- Vote and run for political office in federal and provincial elections.

- Travel outside of Canada with a Canadian passport.

- Enjoy full economic rights.

- Receive pension benefits.

- Enjoy equal treatment and protection under the law without discrimination.

You will be expected to learn, follow, uphold, and obey Canadian laws.

## 3. Embracing Canada

Now that you've adopted Canada as your permanent home, and perhaps have become a citizen, there is no limit to the opportunities you can enjoy thanks to Canada's democratic and multicultural way of life. You will face some challenges along the way, but ultimately, if you remain positive, adapt, and work hard, choosing

Canada as your home will prove to be the best decision you ever made for you and your family.

I hope this book helps you to reach your Canadian dreams! My book *365 Tips for Newcomers: Your First Year in Canada* will continue to help you in your first year. Check out the Self-Counsel Press website (www.self-counsel.com) for more books coming in the future to take your success in Canada to the next level!

# Download Resources

Please enter the URL you see in the box below into your computer web browser to access the download resources.

| **www.self-counsel.com/updates/immigratecan/14kit.htm** |
| --- |

The kit includes websites and other online resources.